Cyrus Hamlin's Civil War

Letters of the
Vice President's Son
on the
Civil War and Reconstruction

David M. Gold

HERITAGE BOOKS
2011

HERITAGE BOOKS

AN IMPRINT OF HERITAGE BOOKS, INC.

Books, CDs, and more—Worldwide

For our listing of thousands of titles see our website
at
www.HeritageBooks.com

Published 2011 by
HERITAGE BOOKS, INC.
Publishing Division
100 Railroad Ave. #104
Westminster, Maryland 21157

International Standard Book Numbers
Paperbound: 978-0-7884-5329-8
Clothbound: 978-0-7884-8764-4

To Dawn

Contents

Illustrations

Preface

Many years ago, while researching the life of John Appleton, Maine's great nineteenth-century chief justice, I came upon the letters of Cyrus Hamlin. The son of Lincoln's first vice president, Hamlin served with Appleton's son as an officer in Brigadier General Daniel Ullmann's brigade of black soldiers during the Civil War. Americans' endless fascination with the Civil War is perhaps sufficient justification to publish another collection of letters by a soldier, but Hamlin had an especially exciting and revealing experience. He chased Stonewall Jackson in the Shenandoah Valley. He commanded a black regiment in Louisiana, struggling against the prejudices of his superiors to obtain equality for his men. Remaining in New Orleans after the war, he took part as a Radical Republican in Reconstruction politics and witnessed the horrific race riot of July 30, 1866. Hamlin seemed headed for a political career when he contracted yellow fever and died within a few days at the age of twenty-eight.

But Hamlin's letters are not just another addition to the enormous corpus of soldiers' testimony on the Civil War. They are uniquely valuable for the light they shed on the history of the Ullmann Brigade. With the exception of the First South Carolina Volunteers, Ullmann's black regiments were the first to be endorsed by the War Department.[1] That endorsement represented a new policy on the part of the government. In 1862, the War Department acknowledged as a fait accompli Major General Benjamin F. Butler's acceptance into service of three regiments of Louisiana Native Guards, militia units originally made up of free blacks enrolled as Confederate forces. It first tried to quash and then finally tolerated the organization by James H. Lane, simultaneously brigadier general and United States senator, of the First Kansas Colored Volunteers. Brigadier General Rufus Saxton had more positive approval from the War Department to raise the First South Carolina Volunteers, but that regiment was an experiment and probably as much a concession to abolitionist opinion as to military necessity. The Ullmann Brigade was both officially sanctioned and unequivocally intended to fill a military need. Whether it was meant to serve garrison duty and thereby free up white troops for combat, the role for black soldiers apparently contemplated by the Emancipation Proclamation, or intended to be a fighting force, as Ullmann and his regimental commanders expected, the brigade represented a new departure for the administration and a major development for the course of the war.

Perhaps because the Ullmann Brigade was slow to organize and never saw significant action, it has received little attention from historians. In the 1880s, black scholars George Washington Williams and Joseph T. Wilson, both Civil War veterans, published histories of the African American troops that contained only fleeting references to Ullmann and his brigade. Among more recent accounts of black soldiers, only Dudley Taylor Cornish's *The Sable Arm* provides more than a mere mention of the brigade. The only substantial report of the Ullmann Brigade's organization and activities is an address to the Maine chapter of the Military Order of the Loyal Legion of the United States by Isaac S. Bangs, a brigade officer, published in 1902. This dearth of attention to the Ullmann Brigade makes Cyrus Hamlin's letters especially noteworthy. They provide unprecedented insight into a neglected chapter of the African American experience in the Civil War.[2]

Hamlin was a lawyer and, according to Bangs, "an officer of fine executive ability."[3] However, he possessed no great intellectual gifts, a fact readily observable in his correspondence. As a boy, he was a mediocre student. During his brief stint in college, Cyrus wrote to his father, "I am not a Grammarian & can not be made one."[4] His spelling was atrocious. Based for a time in Baton Rouge, he repeatedly called the city Barton Rouge. In Hamlin's hands, "position" became "posistion" and "cavalry" became "cavelery." He mangled officers' names, writing, for example, Kio for Cailloux, Holstead for Halsted, and Clousert for Cluseret. He capitalized and punctuated erratically, although in Hamlin's defense it should be said that much better writers of the period also displayed idiosyncrasies in these matters. But Hamlin had his own peculiar manner of taking leave of his correspondents, closing many of his letters with what appears to be "your obj servant" or "your obet son," apparently intending the abbreviation in each instance to mean "obedient." Other closing abbreviations seem to mean "affectionate," although one cannot always be sure.

Hamlin's meaning is almost always readily decipherable, but making out the exact letters or punctuation marks in his correspondence can be tricky. A transcriber can give the benefit of the doubt to a highly literate writer and assume, in questionable cases, that the writer got things right. One can be pretty certain, for example, that Cyrus's older brother Charles spelled words correctly and ended sentences properly. But when a correspondent is as mistake-prone, careless, and inconsistent as Cyrus, the reader of his manuscripts cannot make such assumptions. Left with just the text, one cannot always be sure whether a vowel is an "e" or an "i", when an initial "c" is a capital or just a slightly enlarged lower-case letter, or when a dash is intended as a period. I transcribed the correspondence as precisely as I could, but in many instances another transcriber might well have made other choices.

In those instances where I could not be sure what word Hamlin intended, I put my best guess in square brackets. The word *illegible* in brackets indicates completely indecipherable language. I found it necessary, for the sake of clarity, to employ brackets in other ways, as well: to supply missing letters, especially lower-case R's, which Hamlin often dropped; to flesh out abbreviations; or to identify individuals. Notwithstanding the foregoing warnings about Hamlin's adventures with the English language, readers might be inclined to attribute some eccentricities in the correspondence to editorial or typographical error. Where that seemed to be particularly likely, I inserted "[*sic*]" after the word or phrase in question. In several places, a bracketed date either corrects an error or supplies an omission.

Most of the letters reproduced here are from the Hamlin Family Papers, which are housed at the University of Maine at Orono. The locations of the few letters from other collections are indicated in the endnotes. I am grateful to the New-York Historical Society for permission to reprint Cyrus Hamlin's letter of August 17, 1866, to Daniel Ullmann.

The following abbreviations are used in the endnotes:

HFP   Hamlin Family Papers, Special Collections, Raymond
            H. Fogler Library, University of Maine at Orono
OR   U.S. War Department, *The War of the Rebellion: A
            Compilation of the Official Records of the Union and
            Confederate Armies*, 128 vols. (Washington, D.C.:
            GPO, 1880-1901) (also available at digital.library.cor-
            nell.edu/m/moawar)

I worked on this project in fits and starts from 1980 to 2010, with long years of inactivity in between. During that time, many people responded kindly to my emails and letters of inquiry, some of them so long ago that they have probably retired or moved on to other positions if not other worlds. They worked at the New-York Historical Society, the National Archives and Records Administration, the Fogler Library at the University of Maine at Orono, the United States Army Heritage and Education Center in Carlisle, Pennsylvania, the Williams Research Center in New Orleans, the Hill Memorial Library at Louisiana State University, the New Orleans Public Library, the Louisiana Genealogical and Historical Society in Baton Rouge, the United States Military Academy library, the University of Southern Maine at Portland, the Maine State Archives, and no doubt other places as well. My thanks go to all these institutions and their employees, and to librarians and archivists everywhere, for their unfailing patience, courtesy, and helpfulness.

NOTES

1. The order to Ullmann authorized him to raise a brigade of four regiments, to be recruited in Louisiana. It did not specifically say that the soldiers were to be black, but that was the purpose of the order. *OR*, ser. 3, vol. 3, p. 14; Dudley Taylor Cornish, *The Sable Arm: Black Troops in the Union Army, 1861-1865* (1956; repr., Lawrence, Kan.: University Press of Kansas, 1987), 100-01.

2. George W. Williams, *A History of the Negro Troops in the War of the Rebellion, 1861-1865* (New York: Harper & Bros., 1888); Joseph T. Wilson, *The Black Phalanx: A History of the Negro Soldiers of the United States in the Wars of 1775-1812, 1861-'65* (Hartford: American Publishing Co., 1890); I. S. Bangs, "The Ullman [*sic*] Brigade," in *War Papers Read Before the Commandery of the State of Maine, Military Order of the Loyal Legion of the United States*, 2 (Portland, Maine: Lefavor-Tower, 1902): 289-310.

3. Bangs, "Ullman Brigade," 294.

4. Cyrus Hamlin to Hannibal Hamlin, October 17, 1857, HFP.

Introduction

Cyrus Hamlin was a young man adrift on the eve of the Civil War, more concerned, perhaps, with his own uncertain future than with the fate of the nation. Born in Hampden, Maine, on April 26, 1839, Cyrus had studied law and was just old enough in 1860 to be admitted to the bar. His choice of career may have been inspired by his father's success. Hannibal Hamlin was already a prominent lawyer and politician when Cyrus was born; he would go on to become the most powerful political figure in Maine, a congressman, United States senator, and Abraham Lincoln's first vice president. His political prominence shaped Cyrus's adult life.

Hannibal Hamlin's own father, a prosperous village physician and farmer, died in 1829, leaving Hannibal to run the family farm and dashing his aspirations for a college education. Hannibal tried clerking, surveying, teaching, and running a newspaper before settling on law as a profession. Many young lawyers of the day took part in politics as a way to build up their legal practices, but politics became Hamlin's career. A fervent Democrat and admirer of Andrew Jackson, he represented Hampden in the state legislature from 1835 through 1840 and served for three annual sessions as Speaker of the House. In the 1840s, he twice won election to the U.S House of Representatives, lost a bid for the United States Senate, and returned to the state legislature. In 1848, the legislature chose him to finish the U.S. Senate term of John Fairfield, who died in office, and two years later elected him to a full, six-year term.

For twenty years after his first election to the Maine legislature, Hamlin remained a loyal party man. But Northern Democrats could not agree on the burning issue of slavery, which threatened to tear the party apart. Hamlin was a savvy politician who weighed the political pros and cons of his positions, but there is no question that he sincerely abhorred slavery. As a congressman in the 1840s, he spoke out against the "gag rule" under which the House refused to consider antislavery petitions. During the Mexican War, he actively supported measures to keep slavery out of any conquered territories, and afterwards, with his party bitterly divided, he won election to the U.S. Senate as the candidate of the antislavery Democrats. In the Senate, he witnessed with alarm the repeal of the Missouri Compromise, which had prohibited slavery in the northern part of the Louisiana Purchase, and he condemned the violent attempts of proslavery ruffians to turn Kansas in a slave territory. In 1856, when the Democratic national convention officially adopted the position that Congress had no right to interfere with slavery in the territories, Hamlin wrote to a friend: "The old Democratic party is now only the party of slavery. . . . [T]hat is the standard by which it measures everything and every man! . . . I did not learn my principles, and shall not practice, in that school."[1]

On June 12, 1856, in a dramatic speech to the Senate, Hamlin broke with the Democrats. He pointed out that he had patiently stuck with the party despite its support for measures that had opened the West to slavery. But, he declared, "I have, while temporarily acquiescing, stated here and at home, everywhere uniformly, that when the tests of these measures were applied to me as one of party fidelity, I would sunder them as flax is sundered at the touch of fire. I do it now."[2] Five days later, he attended the first Republican national convention in Philadelphia; in July he accepted the Republican nomination for governor of Maine, and in September won a resounding victory. In February 1857, after forty-nine days in office, he resigned the governorship to accept election by the state legislature to the United States Senate—this time as a Republican. And in 1860, the Republicans nominated Hamlin to run with Lincoln for vice president.

Cyrus Hamlin, a sickly youth of lackluster abilities, grew up in the shadow of this physically robust, politically powerful, self-made man. Hannibal Hamlin hoped that Cyrus would go to college, but, Hannibal wrote to his son Charles, Cyrus "neither studies, reads or writes. His eyes will not admit of it. . . . His health too is not good."[3] Still, Cyrus could have written more often to his father. His neglect in this matter irritated the elder Hamlin. In March 1858, Hannibal did not even know where Cyrus was. "Is he now at Hampden?" he asked Charles. "If so how and what is he doing? If he is there and exercise is what he needs tell him to work a part of each day. He can work on the wood."[4] After Cyrus finished his secondary education at the Fryeburg Academy—he had previously withdrawn from the Bethel Academy after the headmaster complained about his inattention to his studies[5]—Hannibal Hamlin arranged for Cyrus's admission to Waterville (now Colby) College. However, Cyrus dropped out to take up the study of law.[6] In those days, most prospective lawyers, college-educated or not, learned their trade by apprenticing with established practitioners. In 1860, Cyrus had an opportunity to study in the New York City office of a prominent attorney from Maine. Uncertain about his future, Cyrus wrote to his father for advice, a habit he would continue throughout his short life. Hannibal Hamlin's reply, if he wrote one, has been lost, but Cyrus does not seem to have pursued the offer.

In January 1861, Cyrus gained admission to the bar and set up practice in York County. Three months later, the Confederates attacked Fort Sumter. Northerners greeted the outbreak of war with enthusiasm. "From platform and from pulpit," writes historian Ralph Henry Gabriel, "from the coast of Maine to the forests of Minnesota thundered the message: This is a holy war." The "loyal North" could think of nothing but war, wrote a young resident of Providence, Rhode Island; but an event "so hideous . . . in itself" might well "receive such attention when carried on for such noble and just principles as in the present case."[7]

The holy cause was union. During an earlier sectional crisis, Senator Daniel Webster had declaimed for "Liberty and Union, now and forever, one and inseparable." In his inaugural address in 1861, President Lincoln appealed to the "mystic cords of memory" to "swell the chorus of the Union." Many Northerners loved the Union implicitly and responded zealously in its hour of need, while caring little for the plight of African Americans. They thought slavery wrong and opposed its spread, but they were unwilling to fight for black freedom.

After the fall of Fort Sumter in April 1861, Lincoln called for 75,000 state militiamen to augment the small Regular Army for ninety days. The state militias, made up of local volunteer organizations that were better at socializing and politicking than at fighting, proved to be of little use in battle. In May, the president called for 42,000 three-year volunteers, men who would be organized into regiments at the state level but mustered into federal service, and the next month Congress authorized him to raise a half-million troops.

Northern men rallied to the flag from a variety of motives, among them duty, honor, patriotism, religious belief, and ambition. Those from the middle and upper classes often sought officer's commissions, even if they had no military experience. A well-connected man might persuade the state governor to appoint him colonel in a volunteer regiment. More commonly, an aspiring officer would recruit a company of volunteers from his town or county, with the expectation of serving as its captain. Officers of volunteers were usually lawyers, merchants, and other "local worthies" well-known in the community.[8] In the sample he used for a study of soldiers' motivations for fighting, historian James M. McPherson found that 79.6% of white Union officers, but only 24.4% of white enlisted men, worked in professional or white-collar occupations.[9]

John Francis Appleton, a friend of the Hamlins, took the usual path toward officer rank by raising a company of volunteers. A year older than Cyrus, Appleton was the son of a well-known lawyer, legal reformer, and justice of the Maine Supreme Judicial Court. In July 1861, he unsuccessfully sought the assistance of Maine's governor to obtain a commission as a lieutenant. Perhaps his failure was due to the fact that his father, despite

professional prominence and friendship with important politicians, had
no influence outside the world of law. Undaunted, Appleton proceeded to
raise a company for Major General Benjamin F. Butler's planned expedition to Virginia. He placed an ad in a Bangor newspaper calling for
"[a]ble-bodied, intelligent and temperate men" to form a "*crack Company.*" Appleton advertised the pay—thirteen dollars per month plus a
$100 bonus at the end of the war—but he also appealed to the young men
of Maine to "be not unworthy of your Revolutionary sires!" In November,
Appleton was mustered into the service as captain of Company H,
Twelfth Maine Volunteers. Butler's destination having been changed to
New Orleans, the Twelfth Maine set sail on January 2, 1862, for the Gulf
of Mexico.[10]

Cyrus Hamlin had much better connections than Appleton. After
dithering in Maine throughout 1861, raising money to buy socks for Union soldiers and wondering how best to advance his legal career, he finally decided to seek a suitable position in the service. In the spring of
1862, he landed a job as captain and aide-de-camp to Major General of
Volunteers John C. Frémont, a former officer in the Regular Army and
the Republican party's presidential candidate in 1856. Exactly how Hamlin ended up on Frémont's staff is unknown, but it is easy to imagine the
vice president recommending his son to the general, to the secretary of
war, or even to the president of the United States. Few would-be young
officers had that kind of entrée to the top echelons of the political and
military hierarchies. Hamlin would come to appreciate its benefits.

Cyrus was not prime aide-de-camp material. An aide-de-camp had to
receive and transmit orders for his superior, handle correspondence, and
perform other tasks that required an understanding of military organization and events. Hamlin had absolutely no military experience, and even
his writing was seriously deficient. He was, in short, an excellent example of that over-abundant creature of the Civil War, the political officer.
He owed his position to political connections and nothing else. Acquiring
rank through politics did not necessarily portend disaster. As McPherson
has observed, "political generals" sometimes made first-rate commanders,
while graduates of the United States Military Academy could be utter
failures as military leaders.[11] For better or worse, by mid-April, Cyrus the
military novice was in Wheeling, Virginia, with Frémont, preparing for
an expedition to Knoxville, Tennessee.

Fate soon decreed new destinations for the general and his aide.
Frémont's path led to a dead end; his Civil War service terminated with
the Shenandoah Valley campaign of 1862. Hamlin's road led to a reunion
with Appleton in Louisiana, where both young men commanded regiments of the Ullmann Brigade.

NOTES

1. Quoted in Charles Eugene Hamlin, *The Life and Times of Hannibal Hamlin* (1899; repr., Port Washington, N.Y.: Kennikat Press, 1971), 2:286.

2. Quoted ibid., 288.

3. Hannibal Hamlin to Charles Hamlin, July 7, 1857, March 30, 1858, HFP, quoted in H. Draper Hunt, *Hamlin: Lincoln's First Vice President* (Syracuse: Syracuse University Press, 1969), 110.

4. Hannibal Hamlin to Charles Hamlin, March 30, 1858, HFP, quoted in Hunt, *Hamlin*, 110.

5. Cyrus acknowledged that he not been sufficiently studious, but claimed to have worked hard in his last term at Bethel (now Gould) Academy and complained bitterly of mistreatment by Headmaster Nathaniel T. True. Cyrus Hamlin to Charles Hamlin, June 8, 1855, HFP.

6. Cyrus's correspondence suggests that by February 1859, not more than a year and a half after starting at Waterville, Cyrus was back in Hampden preparing for a legal career. Cyrus Hamlin to Hannibal Hamlin, February 14, 1859, HFP.

7. Ralph Henry Gabriel with Robert H. Walker, *The Course of American Democratic Thought*, 3rd ed. (New York: Greenwood, 1986), 119; Nina Silber and Mary Beth Sievens, eds., *Yankee Correspondence: Civil War Letters Between New England Soldiers and the Home Front* (Charlottesville: University Press of Virginia, 1996), 55.

8. Reid Mitchell, *The Vacant Chair: The Northern Soldier Leaves Home* (New York: Oxford University Press, 1993), 23, 47.

9. James M. McPherson, *For Cause and Comrades: Why Men Fought in the Civil War* (New York: Oxford University Press, 1997), 182. McPherson counted officers in the Regular Army as professionals.

10. David M. Gold, "Frustrated Glory: John Francis Appleton and Black Soldiers in the Civil War," *Maine Historical Society Quarterly*, 31 (Summer 1991): 174-204.

11. James M. McPherson, *Battle Cry of Freedom: The Civil War Era* (New York: Oxford University Press, 1988), 328-30.

Chapter One

The War Begins

In December 1860, twenty-one-year-old Cyrus Hamlin was at loose ends. He had settled on law as a profession, but had not yet been admitted to the bar and did not know where he would practice. Until 1859, admission to the Maine bar had been easy. Educational qualifications had been done away with in 1843 as part of a radical democratic attack on the legal profession; all an applicant needed was "good moral character." However, in 1859, the legislature required that the Supreme Judicial Court appoint an examining committee in each county to "examine thoroughly" each candidate for the "requisite legal qualifications." Without a certificate from the committee attesting to his character and qualifications, the candidate could not be admitted to the bar.[1]

That Cyrus had the "requisite legal qualifications" to practice law in 1860 may well be doubted. An aspiring attorney typically apprenticed in the office of a practicing lawyer, and perhaps Cyrus did that. Having been a poor student and a college dropout, though, he still might have been unprepared for the profession. He had an opportunity to either study or work—it is not clear which—in the New York City office of Benjamin F. Mudgett, but seems to have been too insecure to grab it. Cyrus wrote to his father for advice.

Bangor Dec. 4th 1860

My Dear Father.

I received this morning a letter from B.F. Mudgett, which I inclose to you I had some talk with him when I was there I told him I would like much to be there, but made no arrangements of any kind. I do not know what to say or do. I have entertained the idea (with your consent,)—not expecting your aid situated as you are—of applying for one of the Clerkships in the Attorney Generals office, as that would not only be a pecuniary benefit but coming in my profession, & at the end of four years I may have attained a posistion which might be very desirable, if I then wished to persue my profession. I have also thought I would be admitted here in Jan. & go up to Lincoln & settle for a while, as I wish to be doing something & if I go to practising it will be an incentive for me to work. I have sometimes thought this would be the best, for at the end of four years I would have had experience & a profession & not then be oblidged to commence new.

Now Mudgett has written me to come to N.Y. & has made an offer which I think would about pay my board. I would like to go there, & would work for years, if I might stand at last among the first, Otherwise I would not. I have no doubt it is the best place after one obtains a run of practise, but it might take years to acquire it.

I feel that I am only a dependant on you, & that I wish & aught to be doing some thing. & what ever I may do, or which ever way I may turne, it may be the turning point in my life

I desire & wish to be governed by your wishes & advice, what ever it may be, I am satisfied that it will be all for the best. now & for the future.

I understand there will be a trial for a division of the County this Winter.

John Wingate told me he thought of starting a petition to the Legislature to repeal the "Personal Liberty Laws",[2] & that Gen Hersey would head it.

I went to Charlis wedding, had a fine time, the fare cost me seven dollars & ten cts.

your obj son
Cyrus Hamlin

Please to send Mudgetts letter to me again.

C.H.

Cyrus turned down Mudgett's offer and gained admission to the bar in York County in January 1861.[3] It is possible that he had acquired the necessary legal knowledge, but passing the admissions examination would not have been proof. Standard tests did not exist, and examinations were often shams. Charles Francis Adams, just a few years older than Cyrus, was admitted to the Massachusetts bar after "about twenty months of desultory reading" and a short written examination that included several subjects about which he knew nothing. "I was no more fit to be admitted than a child," he recalled. Adams's experience was not uncommon.[4]

The Civil War broke out just three months after Cyrus joined the bar. The historians of Maine's part in the conflict, writing in the glow of victory in 1865, described the zeal with which the people of that state responded to the call to arms.[5] Even allowing for some patriotic exaggeration, it is clear that many young men enthusiastically rushed off to war. Cyrus, however, either did not volunteer or was among those whose ser-

vices the state turned down for the time being because of a surfeit of volunteers. Perhaps his chronic sense of insecurity kept him at home. In any case, he did contribute to the war effort by helping to raise money for supplies for the soldiers. He mentions his earliest activity of record in a letter dated late October 1861. Note also his reference to Maine's coastal defenses. Confederate cruisers had already been operating off the poorly defended New England coast, and people in Maine feared raids on their exposed cities and towns. Governor Israel Washburn, Jr., appointed Vice President Hamlin to a commission to secure the improvement of coastal fortifications. The commission had limited success.[6]

Kittery Oct. 28. 1861.

My Dear Father

The Dr [Augustus C. Hamlin] will probably go to Washington on Thursday, to endeavor to get some more Steamers to build here. He says the Board of Trade at Portland have appointed you to go on, to see about the Defence of our Coast &c. he wishes to know if you are going? if so when? as he wishes to be there at the same time

I have been busy the past week in aiding in a "Levee" in which we have raised two hundred dollars for purchasing Socks &c for our Soldiers

Shall you be at home on Thanksgiven. I shall go East about that time, as I wish to see you all before you leave for W—.

I received a letter from Charley a few days since informing me of my "Uncleship"

I have not yet paid Gilligan. I have paid a note of $45.00 dollars since I have been here, this with my board & winters wood, boots &c have taken all my money. I hope to realize a hundred dollars in a few weeks in some business which I have & then will or any way shall be able to do it before this year passes.

Give my love to all. Mayo is here to work

Your obj son
Cyrus Hamlin

NOTES

1. *Acts and Resolves Passed by the Twenty-third Legislature of the State of Maine, A.D. 1843* (Augusta: William R. Smith, 1843), 49; *Acts and Resolves Passed by the Thirty-eighth Legislature of the State of Maine* (Augusta: Stevens & Sayward, 1859), 112.

2. Personal liberty laws were laws passed in northern states to prevent state officers from enforcing the federal Fugitive Slave Act of 1850. In an attempt to appease the South and head off civil war, some people advocated repeal of the laws. See David M. Gold, "Constitutional Problems in Maine During the Civil War," *Maine Historical Society Quarterly* 22 (Winter 1983): 127-58.

3. H. Draper Hunt, *Hamlin: Lincoln's First Vice President* (Syracuse: Syracuse University Press, 1969), 110; Mark Scroggins, *Hannibal: The Life of Abraham Lincoln's First Vice President* (Lanham, Md.: University Press of America, 1994), 180-81. According to a Hamlin family genealogist, Cyrus was admitted to the bar in 1860 and practiced for a year at Kittery before joining the army. H. Franklin Andrews, *The Hamlin Family: A Genealogy of James Hamlin of Barnstable Massachusetts* (Exira, Iowa: privately published, 1902), 649.

4. Lawrence M. Friedman, *A History of American Law*, 3rd ed. (New York: Simon & Schuster, 2005), 236-37; Charles Francis Adams, *An Autobiography* (Boston: Houghton Mifflin, 1916), 41-42.

5. William E. S. Whitman and Charles H. True, *Maine in the War for the Union: A History of the Part Borne by Maine Troops in the Suppression of the American Rebellion* (Lewiston, Me.: Nelson Dingley Jr., 1865), 1-6.

6. On the defense of Portland, see Louis C. Hatch, ed. *Maine: A History* (1919; repr., Somersworth, N. H.: New Hampshire Pub. Co., 1974), 491-94.

Chapter Two

With Frémont in Virginia

There is a large gap in Cyrus's correspondence after October 1861, but from his father's letters we know that Cyrus was in Washington in February 1862, probably looking for a suitable place in the service. On March 23, Hannibal Hamlin wrote to his son Charles, "Cyrus expects to [be] with Genl Frémont as one of his staff with the rank of Capt. It is not certain but will be determined in a few days." On April 3, Lincoln sent to the Senate a long list of nominees recommended by Secretary of War Stanton as additional aides-de-camp. Cyrus was on the list. Although the Senate did not formally approve the nominations until July, the secretary's recommendation was for practical purposes an appointment. [1]
Cyrus returned to Maine to see his family and his future wife, Sarah Sanborn of Prospect, and then headed for western Virginia to join Frémont.

Assigned to the command of the newly created Mountain Department, Major General John C. Frémont arrived in Wheeling on March 28 with plans for an expedition to Knoxville, through which ran a key rail link between Richmond and the rest of the South. Wheeling was an auspicious place from which to begin a Union campaign. Tucked into the Virginia panhandle between Ohio and Pennsylvania, more than three hundred miles from Richmond, Wheeling was the largest city of a mountainous region where slaves were few and resentment against the planter aristocracy of eastern Virginia ran deep. By the time Cyrus reached Wheeling in the middle of April, northwestern Virginians, meeting in convention, had made clear their intention to separate from the rest of the state.

Cyrus spent the two weeks after his arrival in Wheeling outfitting himself. He wrote several letters describing his trip and circumstances. The vice president's reply to the first of them is one of his few surviving letters to Cyrus.

Head-Quarters, Mountain Department.
Wheeling April 19 1862.

My Dear Father

I arrived here Thursday morn. about eight Oclock although tired & sleepy I immediately reported for duty. My Trunk by some mistake did not get along until yesterday

I am stoping at the McLure House[2] & shall most probably remaine there until we leave here—how long before that time come I am not able to say or ascertain. but I do not believe that we shall leave before ten days at least, it looks as if we will remaine here for weeks, as the mules & horses for transportation are just advertised for (Col Castle master of transportation thinks we shall leave here next week) I have not seen the Gen to advise about my horse. but Col Tracy A.A.G. thinks I had better purchase one = the thing is thus, our staff quartermaster has a requisition for some forty or fifty horses = he is to loan these horse to the members of the Staff & if they wish to purchase they can do so or if they are killed then we have to pay for them (that is each man is responsible for the horse he has, care &c &c) Col Albert[3] says among these horses I may not find one to suit me.

I went & saw Capt Golden yesterday & he said he thought he should have the horses today or the first of next week. I will write you again in a few days about this matter

Love to Mother Sis & Hannie[4]

Saturday was a very warm day here I think I shall get me a thin blue coat & pants besides what I have. I have sixty-four dollars in money which I think will be all I need

Your affec son
Cyrus Hamlin

Bangor Apl 26 1862

My Dr Son

I was glad to receive your letter of the 19th, tho I had before recd a very kind note from Genl Freemont informing me of your safe arrival

I sincerely hope all will go on pleasantly and harmoniously with you and that you will do all you can to that end by a prompt and gentlemanly discharge of all your duties. I have confidence you will do so, and I am sure from the way in which the Genl wrote me, that you will find he too will be kind and friendly to you.

I know Col Tracy well and I think he will cheerfully advise and aid you in your duties. I have heretofore been of service to him.

We have got into our house and find it all very nice. We have not yet all arranged, but are most through and in a few days, all will right.

There is nothing particularly new here. I shall remain at least two weeks more and perhaps three, before I go back. Will let you know when I do go.

We will all be anxious about your health and welfare and you *must not fail* to write at least once a week. Make that a fixed rule & do not depart from it. Let me know all about how you get along.

When I go to Wash. you must write me there as often [*illegible*] the folks at home.

Affec your father
H. Hamlin

Head-Quarters, Mountain Department,
Wheeling April 29 1862.

My Dear Father
I have today purchased me a horse which suits me for one hundred and twenty five dollars & have drawn on mr brown for that sum The note I sent you yesterday you will please distroy & take the inclosed

We are all expecting to leave here tommorrow[5]

Head-Quarters, Mountain Department,
Wheeling April 29, 1862.

My Dear Father
I have this morn. been paid off (up to the 1st of may) it amounted to one hundred & thirty three dollars & some eighty cts. it did not commence until the 5th the time of acceptance. I inclose one hundred dollars hoping it will reach you safely. Had I known I should have been paid I would not have drawn upon Brown. I shall have some thirty dollars left to take with me after all my expenses here. I think this will be as much as I shall require as we go right to camp & draw our rations &c. I have not yet got a servant but have sent for one. I suppose we all leave tonight. Sent our horses this morn.

In haste
Your affec son
Cyrus Hamlin

Upon his arrival in his new department, Frémont had found his troops poorly supplied, spread out over a large, mountainous area, and several thousand fewer in number than expected. Delayed but not deterred from his planned expedition to Knoxville, on May 2 he moved his

*base of operations to New Creek, a railroad depot from which he could
be supplied as he headed south toward Petersburg and Franklin.*

                                        Commissary's Office
                                   New Creek Va. May 3, 1862

My Dear Father,
    While waiting here for my servant to come over after some Coffe
salt, Bacon Beans &c I will improve the time in d[r]oping you a line
    We left Wheeling yesterday about 9. a.m. & arrived here about six
P.m. by special train. Mrs Fremont daughter & son came with us but
went throught to New York Via Baltimore We were not expecting to
leave until Monday or Tuesday although a general order to be in readi-
ness was given a week a go. I left all mess arrangements to be made by
Cap Hopper—we occupy the same tent & mess—but as we left so sudden he failed to procure any thing to eat & should have been without any
thing had I not taken the precaution to have my Haversack a week a go
filled with cheese & crackers—& today I have been busy in getting eati-
bles of the Commissary here— we have one [commissary] attached to the
staff but he is not with us I do not know where he is— I have had to purchase cloth & make bags & have now succeeded in getting a peck of
beans, 2 lbs carrottes, 5 lbs Rice 2 qts Salt, 8 qts Potatoes 3/4 lb Tea, 5
lbs Coffe 6 lbs Salt Pork, 25 lbs Flour, 49 lbs Plot Bread, which I think
will last us until we reach some other Commissary. We purchase all of
our things & do not draw rations, but money for them when we are paid
off. I have to day hired a colord man as my servant. I give him fifteen
dollars per month & board him. Capt Hopper's servant does the cooking
& waiting upon us while my man takes care of the horses & makes himself generaly usefull. Capt H & I have one wall Tent & a servants tent &
one half of a wagon. There are some three thousand Soldiers here one
Ohio & one Va Reg's, some five or six hundred of the German Division
one mountain battery, & 2 Co's of Cavelery. This camp is called Camp
Jissie & a very beautifull one it is, close to the northern branch of the
Potomac & across it is Md. We all expect to leave in the morn, for what
place I do not know. You will please direct in care of Gen at this place,
letters to me
    I rec your letter Friday. The Gen & Col Tracey are very kind to me. I
like very much. I rec a letter from Dr Hamlin he has been sick but will
join us in a few days I am well as ever. I like my horse very much. Love
to all.

                                              Your affec son
                                              Cyrus Hamlin

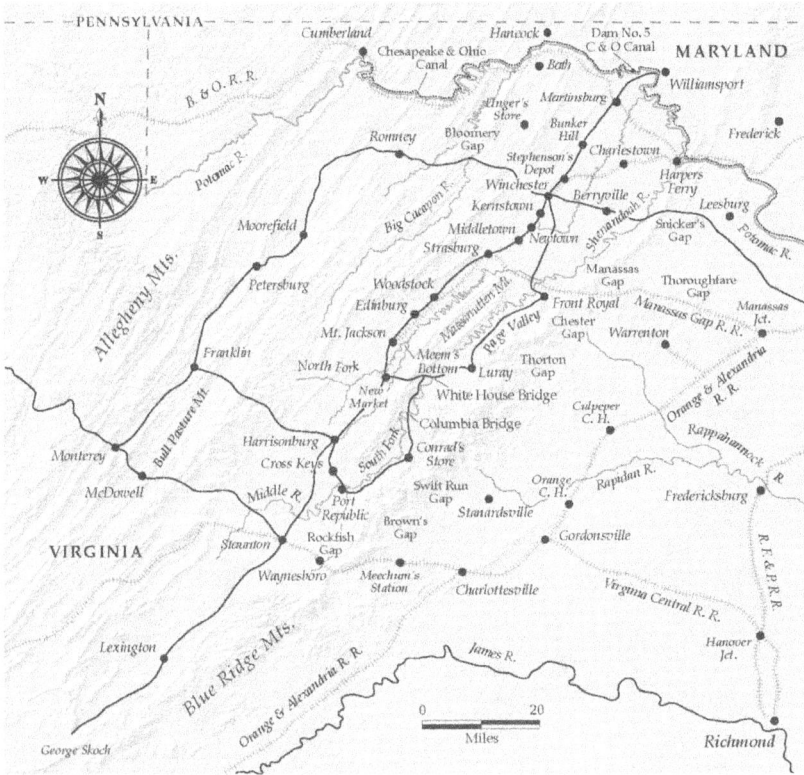

Shenandoah Valley, 1862

From *Shenandoah 1862: Stonewall Jackson's Valley Campaign* by Peter Cozzens. Copyright © 2008 by the University of North Carolina Press. Used by permission of the publisher. www.uncpress.unc.edu

Cyrus served Frémont as acting assistant commissary of subsistence. Colonel Albert Tracy, former adjutant general of Maine and a member of Frémont's staff, described Cyrus in the May 5 entry in his private journal.

May 5th. With the 60th Ohio, some Virginia troops, and a Company of Indiana Cavalry, we leave New Creek, making some eight or ten miles. No Commissary having been attached to Headquarters, I create one out of Captain Cyrus Hamlin—son of my friend, the Senator from Maine. Hamlin having no public money, seizes an ox or two, from a secessionist upon whose farm we encamp, giving the usual voucher—payable by the government, on proof of the loyalty of the secessionist, one of the practical jokes of armies at this time. Next, Captain Hamlin found himself with but one or two assistants, and none of them butchers. So what does our new Commissary do, but take off his own coat, straps and all, and, rolling up his sleeves, go in practically to finish up the job in hand. The result is—beef for the men, and their share thereof, for such officers as care to purchase.[6]

The lack of butchers was the least of the problems facing Frémont's army. The soldiers included German and Italian volunteers, many of little use. They bore antiquated weapons and had a shortage of coats and blankets; many went shoeless. Even food, for both men and horses, was inadequate.

On the evening of May 7, the army reached Petersburg on its southward march through the mountains, while an advance guard of 3,500 men continued on past Franklin. The next day, at McDowell, the small Federal force ran into a Confederate army of 9,000-10,000 under Major General Thomas J. "Stonewall" Jackson, who had been charged with tying up Federal troops in the Shenandoah Valley. McDowell is well south of Petersburg in an area where, on the eve of conflict, pro-Union sentiment could not overcome the fear that the Republican victory in the presidential election of 1860 portended an all-out assault on slavery. After a valiant fight, Brigadier Generals Milroy and Schenk retreated back to Franklin. Cyrus wrote a note to his brother Charlie and a letter to the vice president on May 11 from Petersburg and another letter on May 21, with justifiable bitterness over Frémont's shortage of supplies, from Franklin. The letter of May 11 to Hannibal Hamlin opens with an expression of gratitude for the latter's forgiveness, but with no explanation of what the forgiveness was for.

Petersburg Va. May 11th

My Dear Brother

I send you these two letters & desire you to keep them until my re-turne home—we move to morrow morn at 3.a.m. to Franklin 30 miles from here where Gen Schenk is—he was attacked & had to retire to that place, the German Division reached us to day here Johnson & Lee[7] are there & if they give us a chance we will give them fits they are not probably aware we are here to reinforce Schenk.

In haste
your brother
Cyrus Hamlin

Petersburg May 11, 1862
Near Mid-night

My Dear Father.

I rec your letter & mother's a few days since & it gave me a great deal of pleasure, to know I have your you [sic] forgiveness & that they [sic] past is blotted out with a bright future left.

We are to leave this place in the morn for Franklin 30 miles from here where Gen Schenk is who was attactd & was oblidged to retreat to that place & has orders to fall back upon us if he can not hold it & as we have heard nothing today (I at least) suppose he is there now. The Ger-man Division (the last of them 3 Bidgades) reached us this P.m. there are some Ten thousand of them here 14 Reg's they leave at 3.a.m. & we a 6.a.m. We think we have as large a force as they have & that they are not aware of our presence here. our scouts have been going out for the past three days & most probably we will hear something from them ere morn-ing, if they do not run, we will probably have a brush with them in less than three days— I got a dispatch from the Dr. last night from New Creek—I expect him up to night—Gen Milroy dispatch last night said that some three men of his command were enticed into & [sic] house & while there a man gave a signal & the Bush whackers made a decent & killed two, they beat one of the mens brains out, a party was sent out & the man was killed trying to escape & his house was burnt Tell Mother my Photographs were taken, as I was afraid I would not have an other chance, after I had been out all night returning to Wheeling & I had also been sick a few days before. I have not as yet sent [illegible] one but will do so.

Love to all
Your obj son
Cyrus Hamlin

Franklin, Pendleton Co Va.
May 21. 1862.

My Dear Father

I believe the last time I wrote home we were at Petersburg which we left on monday the 12th & after two days march reached here, & are now waiting for provisions. The enmies force which we expected to meet at McDowell (not laid down on any map we have, is about ten miles south east from Monterey) were the combined forces of Johnson & Jackson. from the best information we get they were from twelve to fifteen thousand, with two twenty four pounders & about thirty five pieces of light artillery. they have retreated & our Scouts say Jackson has gone back to Banks Dept. we lost at the [*sic*] about 30 killed & some 200 wounded, their lost was 45 killed & over 200 wounded but our Scouts report more than that, for they learn that one Regt the 12 Georgia lost 180. The Union men here are quite numerous just now, whether it is because our forces are here or from a conviction of the right I can not judge yet[8] I have no doubt there are many who will be true to us. many men are deserting them there are probably over one hundred here in this County who have come home they say there are many yet to come as well as many to come over if they ever give us a chance to have an engagement with them. The whole route to this place has been mostly in the Vallies, mountains on either side. It is a sad sight to follow after such an army as this, for where we camp there is no fences left & on the road, all kinds of animals have to take their chances. I often turne my back upon such things, for I think I have cause to complaine against the course of the Govt. for a while I done the business of Chief Commissary—for the last four days the men have not had rations—full rations have not been given out at any time—yesterday 1/28 of a ration was given out to this army dont know the force but judge some fifteen thousand men. only think of this, there is Fresh Beef but no salt—Gen Fremont asked or made a requisition for horses &c the first of Feb—& now while in the field has not been yet furnished enough to feed his men one day & it is only seventy two miles to the rail road, our baggage teams are employed to get forage for the army, when we get ten days rations for a surpluse we shall leave here, when that day comes I can not tell, but hope soon. The Dr. reached us on Tuesday last. he has been assigned to Col Clouseret Brigade which is in the advance. There are but a very few Slaves in this part of the State & these are leaving. Many men here are as strong against the institution as myself This is place is the County seat & contains some thirty or fourty buildings, one meeting house formely some three or four stores which done quite an extensive business. As near as I can ascertain I judge we are going to Stanton, if so, I hope to get in to Washington to see you.

Love to all.—
Your affc son
Cyrus Hamlin
Direct to New Creek as usual

Cyrus overstated Jackson's numbers, a common mistake among Jackson's adversaries, but his estimate of casualties was reasonably accurate. The Confederates won the battle by forcing a Union retreat, but they suffered 116 killed and three hundred wounded to the Union's thirty-four killed and 220 wounded.

On May 23, Jackson surprised and crushed a Union garrison at strategically located Front Royal and over the next two days fought Major General Nathaniel P. Banks successfully down the Valley Pike to Winchester. On May 24, President Lincoln ordered Major General Irvin McDowell to transfer two divisions from Fredericksburg, midway between Washington and Richmond, to the valley to hit Jackson's flank. Frémont received orders to march eastward from Franklin to Harrisonburg and attack Jackson from the rear, and it was hoped that Banks would regroup and pursue Jackson from the north. Frémont with fifteen thousand men (at least on paper) and Brigadier General James Shields with McDowell's ten thousand sought to converge near Strasburg to cut off Jackson's escape. But Shields tarried and Frémont, instead of going to Harrisonburg, embarked on a long, slow detour that looped northward back through Petersburg. Jackson slipped through Strasburg untouched. Historians have charged Frémont with ineptitude, attributing his costly detour to minor obstacles in the mountain passes. Colonel Tracy, however, wrote that the poorly provisioned army, its miseries increased by downpours, floods, lack of forage, and inadequate transportation, had to double back to Petersburg and its supply line. Cyrus saw matters in the same light.

Petersburg Va. [May] 26th 1862

My Dear Father

We arrived here about 4.P.M. from Franklin. We are on our way to cut off (I think) Jackson whome we understand is pushing Banks & has possession of Martinsburg. this Dept is clear now they having left there may perhaps have left a rear guard I think the Gens plan was to cut a cross from F—, but as I stated to you before the want of transportation has compelled us to come here in order to get provissions, we take 5 days rations here—& the County (if they do not run) will hear from us I rec your letter by Capt Wood this Eve, with also two letters from Sis. I think we leave here early in the morn via Morefield & shall make force marches as we have yesterday & today, had we had sufficent transportation the rebels would never have reached Martinsburg for we would have followed them so fast that we would have got them but as it is we have kept advised of their movements but hunger compelled us to halt. Our paymaster who has been with us all the time leaves tomorrow morn for Wheeling & as he will not reach us until the first of June, he has paid me off $148.00 & [*illegible*] as I have an opportunity to send you $100, I improve it

I am well

In haste your obj son
Cyrus Hamlin

P.S.
I send this by Hon G. W. Wright who leaves for Washington in the morn

C.H.

Frémont finally approached Strasburg on June 1 and turned south, west of Massanutten Mountain and the Shenandoah River, in pursuit of Jackson. Shields headed up the Luray Road, east of the river, with the idea of cutting off Jackson's retreat through one of the gaps in the Blue Ridge Mountains. Jackson slowed Shields down, and kept him from uniting with Frémont, by sending cavalry to burn bridges over the Shenandoah's South Fork. Cyrus, meanwhile, anticipated an eventual confrontation with the Confederates and his own possible death. His letter, dated June 1, 1862, had the note dated two days later appended to it.

Camp 4 miles from
Strausburg June 1st 1862.

My Dear Father
I rec your letter of the 25th this Eve.
We arrived here at ten A.M. & occupy a hill which reaches across the Valley, with our whole force except one Brigade which was sent in advance to draw the enemy out Col Clousret in Command (Dr is with him) our rear or re-enforcement consists of two Brigades of German Gen Blenker in Comd. we had six men wounded by shells not dangerous—we waited quietly with our artillery bearing on the roads (two) but they have retreated, we were to attack them this P.M. but they have retreated—a

cavelry man has just come in & says our cavelery, which went out to see which way they have retreated have been taken with two Regs of Infantry—the Bugle has sounded & perhaps we are going to move so I will close I sent you one hundred dollars by George W. Whight which I hope will reach you safely. What money I send you in case of my death you will please give Miss Sanborn. We have had hard marches to this place over mountains it has rained most every day. last night very hard. Good night

> In haste
> Your affec son
> *Cyrus Hamlin*

> Tuesday 3 of June
> 4 miles from Woodstock

We attacked & routed the rear guard yesterday. Last night Sam Fessenden came up with Capt Hall of 2 Maine Battery. Tell his Father he is well. The Hamlin Battery is up under Lt Mayo & whether I shall try & see them to day We start in persuit again this morn. We have 150 prisoners. Shields we are in hopes is ahead of them if so, we have them. We had two men killed & our Chief of Artillery slightly wounded I shall [*illegible*] the Maine Cavelery I will [write] again soon.

On June 5, Hannibal Hamlin brought his wife up to date on what he had learned about Cyrus's performance as a soldier.

The letter you sent me from Cyrus was duly recd. and I have another several days later. He is well, contented & in good spirits. The troops under Freemont are now in active service, and I cannot help feeling keenly anxious about him. Providence can only tell what I may hear at any hour. it may be of his wounds or his death. I try to be reconciled as I know he is doing his duty. May God protect him and return him to us in health.

I am gratified to learn that he is giving his Genl Satisfaction. I yesterday recd a letter from *one who knows* & that letter says:

"It would gratify you to know, not only how much your son is liked by the young officers of the Staff, but what fine young men whose regard is worth having, they are. Before I left Wheeling Capt Hamlin was one of four whom the Genl was sure needed no second explanation and who never by any chance got out of favor. I as his oldest and hardest worked Secretary knew how much merit it required to meet all the Genls re-

quirements and it was a great pleasure to find [in] Capt Hamlin the feeling of personal interest which made his power to be useful, so agreeable.
The Staff of the Genl are true friends and brothers to each other"

It is gratifying indeed to learn that Cyrus is giving so good satisfaction.

*The separated Union armies hoped to converge on Jackson below
Massanutten Mountain. On June 8, five thousand rebel soldiers under
Major General Richard Ewell intercepted Frémont and his ten thousand
men at the hamlet of Cross Keys, west of the river, and inflicted 684
casualties (including men taken prisoner) while themselves suffering 288
wounded and killed. It was the only time during Jackson's valley campaign that Confederate forces were outnumbered at the moment of battle,
but Frémont, according to his detractors, made up for that deficiency by
his incompetence. (Frémont's defenders have pointed to the wretched
condition of his army.) That night, Ewell took most of his men across the
river and rejoined Jackson. The next day, the Rebels defeated Shields's
stubborn but vastly outnumbered army near Port Republic. They kept
Frémont from joining the fray by burning the only bridge across the un-
fordable North River, which joined the South Fork at Port Republic. With
this battle, Jackson's valley campaign came to an end. By June 12, Frémont and Shields had both turned north. Jackson, having tied up Union
divisions badly needed in the East, procured supplies, and taken thousands of prisoners, headed southwest toward the safety of Staunton, Virginia.*

*Cyrus survived Cross Keys without harm. Biographical notices of
Cyrus state that his conduct during the battle received Frémont's favorable attention, but no source is ever given. The story may have been told
first in the announcement of Cyrus's death in the* New Orleans Republican *in 1867. The writer claimed to have made Cyrus's acquaintance at
Cross Keys and recalled "a favorable mention of him from his general to
us personally, shortly after the severest part of the engagement had taken
place."[9] What Cyrus actually did at Cross Keys, however, remains a mys-
tery.*

*Soon after the fight, Cyrus obtained leave to visit Washington. With
the battle behind him, high spirits replaced gloomy foreboding—
Hannibal Hamlin reported to his wife that he had seen Cyrus in "excellent health & spirits"[10]—but the dissolution of the Mountain Department
at the end of June placed Cyrus in a quandary. Lincoln consolidated the
forces of Frémont, Banks, and McDowell into the new Army of Virginia,
commanded by Frémont's junior in rank, Major General John Pope. But
Frémont despised Pope and gave up his command rather than serve un-*

der him. Colonel Tracy wrote: "All the hours of worriment and toil, and all the days and nights of marching, all the brunt of the elements or of the bullets, were to count as nothing. And even the pursuit, with the escape of Jackson solely through the admitted and recorded fault of others—was to be held upon our part, as but a blameful failure! A sense of the bitterness of the injustice done, pervaded us all."[11]

NOTES

1. *Senate Executive Journal,* 37th Cong., 2d sess., July 17, 1862, 425, 433-34.

2. The McLure (also spelled McClure) House Hotel opened in 1852 and is still in business.

3. Hamlin probably meant to write "Col Tracy."

4. Cyrus Hamlin's stepmother Ellen Emery Hamlin (1835-1925), sister Sarah Jane Hamlin (1842-1878), and half brother Hannibal Emery Hamlin (1858-1938). Although he called her "mother," Ellen was only a few years older than Cyrus.

5. The rest of this letter is missing.

6. Francis F. Wayland, ed., "Frémont's Pursuit of Jackson in the Shenandoah Valley: The Journal of Colonel Albert Tracy, March-July 1862," *Virginia Magazine of History and Biography* 70 (April 1962): 170. Frémont officially made Cyrus acting commissary of subsistence on May 6, 1862. Cyrus still held the position as of June 25. General Order No. 23, Cyrus Hamlin Staff Officer's File, National Archives and Records Administration, Washington, D.C.; *OR,* ser. 1, vol. 12, pt. 1, p. 35.

7. Hamlin might have been thinking of Confederate Generals Joseph E. Johnston (1807-1891), who in May 1862 was in command of the Department of Northern Virginia, and Robert E. Lee (1807-1870), who had been called to Richmond as military advisor to Confederate president Jefferson Davis. Neither Johnston nor Lee was near Franklin on May 11, as reported in Hamlin's letter. It is possible that "Johnson" refers to Confederate Brigadier General Edward Johnson.

8. Franklin, situated close to the future border between West Virginia and Virginia, was far more sympathetic than Wheeling to the Confederate cause. Oren F. Morton, *A History Pendleton County West Virginia* (Franklin. W. Va.: privately published, 1910), 107-16. This no doubt explains Cyrus's uncertainty regarding the motives of local inhabitants who professed loyalty to the Union.

9. *New Orleans Republican,* August 29, 1867.

10. Quoted in H. Draper Hunt, *Hamlin: Lincoln's First Vice President* (Syracuse: Syracuse University Press, 1969), 252n73.

11. Wayland, "Journal," 352.

Chapter Three

Interregnum

Frémont returned to his home in New York accompanied by his staff to await further developments. He did not know it at the time, but for him the war was over. He had caused trouble for Lincoln, first with his association with crooked contractors and with unauthorized, extreme anti-slavery measures while in charge of the Department of the West in 1861[1] and then with his military failures in the Shenandoah Valley. In 1864, Frémont accepted the presidential nomination of a convention of abolitionists committed to a vigorous prosecution of the war and a radical reconstruction of the South. However, he withdrew from the race after the Democrats nominated former Major General George B. McClellan and called for an end to the war and reunion without the abolition of slavery. With his withdrawal, Frémont's public career came to an end.

In the meantime, as a staff was of little use without an army, Frémont assigned his aides to other generals; Cyrus, he thought, ought to serve with Banks. Cyrus declined the suggestion and spent the second half of 1862 wondering what to do with himself. He remained in touch with Frémont, apparently hoping that his former boss would get a new command. He pondered the possibilities of positions with other generals, at least one of which he sought to obtain through his political connections. He tried to get involved in a potentially lucrative legal claim against the government, half-heartedly joined the staff of Governor Washburn of Maine to help recruit soldiers, and, as usual, wrote to his father for advice. The one big step Cyrus took was getting married.

New York June 30. 1862

My Dear Father,

I reached here yesterday & found I could not go on until night & so I went & made a call on Mrs Fremont who informed me that the Gen would be here to day so I concluded to remaine here & see him. I called on him this P.M. & as there were quite a number present I did not have a chance to talk with him as I wished & I was unwilling as well as himself to let other people hear it. he said he had assigned many of the Staff to other Gens & he thought me to Genl Banks. I thanked him but told him I prefered to remain with him & what ever course he persued I would stand by him—I think he said that most probably he should leave the Service—I have got permission to go to the Army & get my baggage & returne here. I shall take one of my horses—my gray one certainly as far as Washington & if I am to returne home—I shall take her too!

I wish to know what I had better do—had I better stay with the Genl until mustered out of service? Do you think I had better join any one else?—or Had I better ask the Sec of War to give me a commission in the Regular Army? My own mind dictates me to stay with the Genl & if he leaves, then to returne home. I think I prefer this, however I wish you to advise me fully upon this subject & what ever you think best will be so. If you will write me fully upon this subject & Washington at the Washington house, as I will returne there after getting my baggage. Rumors here we have Richmond I hope so whether so or not.

In haste
Your [*illegible*] son
Cyrus Hamlin

A few days later, Cyrus was in Washington. The vice president had gone back to Maine to do some politicking and to call, publicly as well as privately, for using black men "in all possible way[s] to relieve our soldiers."[2] Cyrus was still anxiously awaiting his father's counsel. Perhaps following Hannibal Hamlin's lead, Cyrus, for only the second time in his correspondence (see his letter of May 21, 1862), expressed his abhorrence of slavery. This time, he hinted at the need to recruit and arm black soldiers. It is impossible to know the depth of Cyrus's commitment to the cause of black freedom as of mid-1862. Nearly five dozen letters written by the teenaged Cyrus to his father and brother survive, but few indicate a serious interest in politics or the plight of the slaves. In 1855, he heard the great abolitionist William Lloyd Garrison lecture on slavery and free religion, but in a letter to Charles he commented only on the latter. The next year, when Hannibal Hamlin was running for governor of Maine, Cyrus proudly wrote how a campaign orator had been interrupted by wild applause upon declaring that the candidate had always been for freedom and against the extension of slavery. Two days before the 1856 presidential election, Cyrus took part in a four-and-a-half hour political debate in which he had taken the Republican side. He informed Charles that he had "whipped [his opponent] all to pieces and got the decision of the Presdant and the Audience." In all his other letters before May 1862, he said nothing about slavery.[3]

Washington July 6. 1862

My Dear Father

When I arrived here Mr Deering told me concerning the Telegraph Dispatch, with the hope ere this that I would receive a reply from my letter written at New York I have waited until now. I have been greatly at loss what to do, for if I accepted a possistion upon the Staff of Gen. Pope it would look as if I did not indorse the course of Gen Fremont & I cannot in my conduct do that which would disprove his course.

After waiting & thinking the matter all over I yesterday made up my mind that I would try & obtaine a place on Gen Wool's Staff. I have thought this best as he will have a large Camp of Instruction & it will give me an opportunity to learn as well as study the art of war. I do not desire to fight for the institution of slavery & it seems to me that our armies are doing it, for except Gen Hunter there is not one in the field holding a command but what is committed to the Pro Slavery creed I am very much disappointed in the course of the Administration in many respects. I think no man what ever may be his color who is aiding in this rebellion but should suffer the consequences. I hope there will be a change for the better certainly it can not be much worse. With the course, being persued, I think it will be hard to find more men in New England

I have in the morning to get my horses & baggage if I can find them & shall return here in the meantime Messrs Brown & Deering will secure the influence of Senators Harris, King, Lane Morrill &c nothing yet has been said to Gen Wool but they are to write him upon the subject. If you think it consistant with your views I would like for you to write the Gen upon the Subject. I shall apply for a Maj Commission I would like you to write me upon this subject

Give my love to all

Your [*illegible*] son
Cyrus Hamlin

P.S.

I heard to day that Lt Col Varney & Adj Mudgett of the 2^d were both wounded & taken prisoners also Capt Emerson of the same is dead.[4] I also learn that thirty-thousand of Buell's army reached Fortress Monroe to day[5]

C.H.

Cyrus's letter revealed a nascent commitment to the abolition of slavery, which may have been fostered by association with Frémont. Frémont had been the Republican Party's first nominee for president and, as noted above, had antagonized Lincoln with his radical antislavery position early in the war. Cyrus's budding idealism would bear fruit six months later. In the meantime, he had a more immediate problem: What to do?

Washington July 14 [15]. 1862.

My Dear Father

I have been to Front Royal but did not succeed in finding anything but my trunk my horses (2) are with the Dr. one has been stolen.

I wrote the Gen a few days since but have not rec an ans but Mr Boggs has been to see him & he is to have a command I do not know where. I went this morn to see the Sec of War & I had a very pleasant interview, he said he had been expecting to hear from or see me before he said he would assign me to any Gen's staff I might wish—I told him I had been thinking I would like to go to the Camp of Instruction with Gen Wool—he said I should—I also said I had been thinking that I would like to go to "Maine" & aid Gov Washburne in mustering & raising the new troops. he siad I might do so. He also gave me an order for transportation to Warrenton to get my horses &c & I shall leave immediately for that place—. I hope to be in Maine soon & then I can tell what's best to do for the future.

Your affec son
Cyrus Hamlin

P.S.

I did not tell or say that you wished me to go on Wool's Staff—it was the Sec offer voluntary.

C.H.

Hannibal Hamlin had worked closely with General Wool in 1861 organizing the transportation of troops from New York City to Washington.[6] Cyrus never did join up with Wool, though, and Stanton ordered Cyrus to Maine to assist Governor Washburn.

Washington July 23. 1862.

My Dear Father

Since writing you last I have been to Sperryville Va. & got two of my horses & have them here. I have been to the War Dpt & have orders to report to Gov Washburne— to do what ever I may be able to help raise our quota of troops—I hope I may find some thing that will keep me in Maine at least a month— Sec Stanton has been very kind to me & I shall always feel under great obligations to him—he will assign me to duty after I get th[r]ough in Maine upon any ones staff that I may wish to go. I shall leave tomorrow with my horses for Maine where I hope to be by the 30[th] I am very sorry to learn that Charlie has taken a Maj's Commission or that he is going at all. I wish he would stay at home. Love to all.

Your obj son
Cyrus Hamlin

When Cyrus heard in October that Frémont might be given a new command, he asked Governor Washburn to release him from his duties in Maine, apparently as state mustering officer,[7] so that he might join his old commander in New York.[8]

[Bangor October 2, 1862]

Dear Sir,

I desire to join Gen. Frémont in New York as there seems to be a prospect of his having a command.

If you have no further duty for me, please give me an order to report to the Sec. of War.

I wish to stop in Boston a few days, so that I have left the date blank, & will fill it up.

[Cyrus Hamlin]

Before leaving for New York, Cyrus married Sarah Sanborn in Prospect, Maine. She accompanied Cyrus on his travels. While at loose ends in New York, Cyrus saw an opportunity to use his legal training in the long-running dispute between partners Edward H. Carmick and Albert C. Ramsey and the U.S. government stemming from the government's abrogation of Carmick and Ramsey's contract to carry the mail from the East to San Francisco.[9] His participation in the case promised to be profitable, but the prospect of the vice president's son representing claimants against the government raised ethical and political questions. As a subsequent letter reveals, the Hamlins did get involved in trying to settle the claim, Cyrus dealing with the client and Hannibal with Secretary of the Treasury Salmon P. Chase.

No 238. Henry St.
Brooklyne Nov 18./62

My Dear Father.

I intended to have written home ere this but hoped to hear from you at home before I wrote again We are as yet stopping here as I am with Gen F— & shall remaine with him—certainly until I see you again. Gen

has been to Washington & had an interview with the President all I have
heard, is, that it was very satisfactory & he feels very much pleased about
it—I have not been over to day as it rained but shall go over tomorrow as
I supposed he returned last night. I go into see Charles H Farley every
time I am over, through him—I am not known in the case—I have secured a claim to prosecute—perhaps you may know about it—Carmick
& Ramsey mail contractors of the overland route to San Francisco It
seems that the Post Master Genl. abrogated the Contract & Congress past
a bill for their relief—but other Dpt. interfeared or caused it not to be
settled. I do not fully understand the thing yet as I have only the paper I
inclose to you as yet—but expect the papers every day. It seems the past
administration would never do anything. In 1858 House Judiciary Com-
mitte reported Congress has done everything it can & it is the duty of the
1st Comptroller to settle it—& Mr Whittlesey says it ought to be done in
a report he makes. I do not, as I said before know much about it, but this
outline. Farley is to have twenty five thousand dollars to get it settled &
out of it he gives me twenty of it. I want your opinion whether I better go
into it—that is if every thing is all right & honorable. I think it can be
done with a little assistance & if so it is certainly worth trying for. When
do you leave for Washington I shall by that time have all the papers &
will submit them to you. I want you to remaine here one day on your way
for this purpose & if practible I can go to Washington with you.

We have a good boarding place & I spend to most of my time at
home. Sarah sends her love to all.

Your affectionate son
Cyrus Hamlin

P.S.
        Send me the report back

C.H.

*Cyrus's correspondence does not indicate whether he played any
further role in attempting to settle Carmick and Ramsey's claim. The
partners' attorneys later contended in court that Elisha Whittlesey, First
Comptroller of the Treasury, had been prepared to settle the claim for
$185,000 before he suddenly died in 1863. Carmick and Ramsey ac-
cepted an offer of $43,830.04 from Whittlesey's successor, then sued for
more. In 1866, the United States Court of Claims denied them relief.*[10]

NOTES

1. Frémont had declared the slaves of rebellious Missourians emancipated. Lincoln modified Frémont's proclamation by restricting it to slaves who had directly aided the Confederate cause, thus conforming it to an act of Congress passed a few weeks earlier.

2. Quoted in Mark Scroggins, *Hannibal: The Life of Abraham Lincoln's First Vice President* (Lanham, Md.: University Press of America, 1994), 184. See Charles Eugene Hamlin, *The Life and Times of Hannibal Hamlin* (1899; repr., Port Washington, N.Y.: Kennikat Press, 1971), 2:438.

3. Cyrus Hamlin to Charles Hamlin, March 18, 1855, November 2, 1856, HFP; Cyrus Hamlin to Hannibal Hamlin, July 12, 1856, ibid.

4. Cyrus was mistaken about Emerson. Varney, Mudgett, and Emerson were taken prisoner at Chickahominy on June 27, 1862, during the Seven Days' Battles in eastern Virginia. William E. S. Whitman and Charles H. True, *Maine in the War for the Union: A History of the Part Borne by Maine Troops in the Suppression of the American Rebellion* (Lewiston, Me.: Nelson Dingley Jr., 1865), 48. All three were exchanged for Confederate prisoners in August 1862. *CWD*

5. On July 6, 1862, when Hamlin reported that Major General Don Carlos Buell's troops had reached Fortress (or Fort) Monroe in Virginia, Buell was actually in Tennessee marching his Army of the Ohio toward Chattanooga.

6. Scroggins, *Hannibal*, 170; H. Draper Hunt, *Hamlin: Lincoln's First Vice President* (Syracuse: Syracuse University Press, 1969), 151-52.

7. *OR*, ser. 3, vol. 2, p. 293.

8. Cyrus Hamlin to Israel Washburn, Jr., October 2, 1862, formerly located in Civil War Correspondence—Governor, vol. 42, p. 26, Maine State Archives, Augusta (now untraceable following a reorganization of the archives). The transcription given here is from my notes.

9. The overland mail route referred to by Cyrus in his letter of November 18, 1862, was the Acapulco, Vera Cruz, and San Francisco route. Congress passed an act to settle Carmick and Ramsey's claim, but the Treasury Department refused to pay. See *Post Office Appropriations Act*, 11 Stat. 94 (1856) , § 6; S.R. 22, 36th Cong., 1st sess., April 4, 1860.

10. *Carmick and Ramsey Case*, 2 Ct. Cl. 126 (1866).

Chapter Four

Organizing the Ullmann Brigade

Frémont never received a call from the War Department to return to duty, and Cyrus seems to have been in limbo for the remainder of 1862. His break came with the Emancipation Proclamation on January 1, 1863. The story goes that one night in January 1863, Vice President Hamlin received a visit from Cyrus and several other army officers, who urged him to persuade Lincoln to arm the blacks. Hamlin had already been pressing the necessity of this step and had shown Lincoln letters from Cyrus praising the Negro's fighting potential. Hamlin brought the officers to see the president the next day. Moved by the young men's enthusiasm and willingness to lead, Lincoln agreed that the time had come at last. He immediately drew up an order to Secretary of War Edwin M. Stanton to organize a black brigade to be led by white officers. Vice President Hamlin personally delivered the order to Stanton, and Stanton directed Colonel Daniel Ullmann, a New York politician who had been paroled after being taken prisoner at the Battle of Cedar Mountain, to proceed with the task.

The tale of the visit to Lincoln has been recounted in various sources, but it probably originated with the recollections of an elderly Hannibal Hamlin.[1] It may or may not have occurred as Hamlin remembered. One thing is certain: Lincoln did not authorize the arming of black men just because Hannibal and Cyrus Hamlin asked him to. The vice president had no sway with Lincoln, and pressure to use black troops had been coming from other, more influential sources. Demands for the recruitment of black soldiers had been growing through 1862, especially in New England. Chief Justice John Appleton of Maine wrote to U.S. senator William Pitt Fessenden "that our only hope of success is in arming the black man as well by way of terror to the master as for the sake of the efficient aid they are capable of rendering in the field." Governor Washburn noted "one full chorus of inquiry," including even the most conservative citizens, asking why Maine had to send her noble young men, "the strength, hope & ornament of the State, to be cut down by the thousands by the deadly malaria of a Southern summer when the Govt could use in their stead, men acclimated loyal, & willing."[2]

Cyrus's own letter to his father of January 25, 1863, throws a shadow over the story of the young officer's visit to Lincoln. Cyrus was in New York with Ullmann on that date, but his letter suggests that he had merely been considering the idea of leading black troops, and not with any enthusiasm. And it would seem from Hannibal Hamlin's recommendation of Appleton's son for colonel of the "Maine" regiment that the vice president had no idea his son was interested in Ullmann's project.

As noted in the Introduction, attempts to create black fighting forces had been made before in parts of the occupied South. In the spring of 1862, in the Sea Islands off South Carolina, Major General David Hunter formed the First South Carolina Colored Regiment, but his coercive recruiting measures and opposition from the administration in Washington led to its disbandment later that year. In August, Brigadier General Rufus Saxton picked up where Hunter had left off, but despite some initial success, progress was slow. At Camp Parapet in Louisiana, Brigadier General John Phelps tried to form regiments from the slaves pouring into the camp, but Butler, in command of the Department of the Gulf, would not let him proceed without War Department authorization. However, Butler, with the War Department's acquiescence, did accept the 2,700 black men, free and slave, of the First, Second, and Third Louisiana Native Guards.

Although the Emancipation Proclamation declared that freed slaves would be received into the armed forces to garrison forts and man vessels, Ullmann, newly promoted to brigadier general, expected his soldiers to fight. He wanted officers who were ready, willing, and able to stand up to racial prejudice in the army, to train raw black recruits, and to lead their men in battle. Social respectability and military experience would be useful attributes in such officers, but not more useful than dedication to the cause of the black combat soldier. Ullmann's brigade, fully endorsed by the War Department, was to consist of four regiments (later expanded to five), the officers to be selected in cooperation with the governors of Maine, Massachusetts, and New York. Ullmann asked the vice president to recommend someone for colonel of the "Maine" regiment. Hamlin named Captain John F. Appleton of Bangor, who, he said, had "acquitted himself well and bravely in the service."[3] As we will see, that recommendation caused some complications in the organization of the brigade.

White officers had varied motives for seeking positions in black regiments. Robert Gould Shaw, the high-born colonel of the Fifty-fourth Massachusetts Volunteers, reluctantly accepted the command from a sense of noblesse oblige. Thomas Wentworth Higginson, also born to a wealthy Massachusetts family, was a foremost abolitionist who jumped at the chance to lead the First South Carolina Volunteers (Colored) in a

fight for freedom. Many other officers of black regiments had a less hon-
orable motive: rank ambition. Ullmann noted acidly "how jaundiced eyes
were cleared to see Colored Troops only in rainbow tints, when Commis-
sions in the Field, Staff and Line began to flutter in the air, thickly as
autumn leaves."[1]

Cyrus Hamlin nursed a growing sense of self-importance and enti-
tlement that his father, for all his political ambition, seemed to lack. Per-
haps Cyrus acquired it from Frémont, who possessed an outsized ego
and a boundless drive for personal advancement. Whatever its source,
Cyrus's passion for recognition and position swelled during the war. At
the same time, though, his commitment to the cause of black soldiers also
deepened. At first, he hesitated to accept Ullmann's offer of a colonelcy
because of the "social & political bearing" it might have. (His lack of
experience as a combat officer seems not to have troubled him.) Until
Northerners overcame their view of Africans as a degraded race, being
an officer in a black regiment meant inviting opprobrium from inside the
army and from society at large. Experience with blacks as comrades in
arms induced many white soldiers to change their tune, but not all; even
the abolitionist Higginson retained a condescending, paternalistic view
of blacks. Cyrus, though, from the limited evidence in his letters, seems to
have grown into a warm advocate of racial equality.

Brooklyn Jan 25/63.
238 Henry St.

My Dear Father

I received your letter a few days since. I concluded not to Ans. it until I had seen Gen U—which I did yesterday I have been thinking the
subject over—that as I learn that there is a bill before Congress to cut off
the pay of those not on duty it might be well for me to look about to see
what & where I might go. I have had some thoughts about (before hear-
ing from you) asking for power to raise a Colord Reg. & more than once
I have thought of asking your advice. not about my competency—but
about the social & political bearing in the future— Gen U— asked me if
I would accept a Lt Col's posistion. I told him I could not, as the
posistion I now held I considered better & that I must do justice to myself,
& as I saw no chance for promotion except in removal, resignation, or
death of the superior I could not accept any thing less than Col. When he
said, that you desired as he had alloted but one Reg to Maine that Johny
Appleton should have that place but perhaps he would accept the Lt Col.
& I might have the Col. I said no that in that case it might compromise
you & if you desired Appleton to have the Col.ship I must consider myself out & could not accept it after knowing this He said he desired me to

go & I must go with him & he said, Well I will assign to Regs to Maine & you shall have one & Appleton the other. I thought it best then to accept it, but since have had some question about it. I desire your advice about it—If I had better retract my consent telegraph me ("not to accept") I suppose you are acquainted that the destination of the Brigade will be *New Orleans*, which is to be kept Secret. So far as the ability & responsibility I have not fear that I am competent, therefore I do not wish you to let this trouble you in your decision.

Your obj son
Cyrus Hamlin

The confusion over command is reflected in Ullmann's letter to Hannibal Hamlin the next day. "After writing to you on Saturday I saw Capt. Hamlin and he consented to take a Colonelcy," Ullmann wrote. "Do I understand you to say that he has changed his mind? I have a very satisfactory letter from Gov. Coburn. He is very hearty in his co-operation." Governor Abner Coburn of Maine objected to Appleton on grounds of youth and inexperience, even though Appleton was slightly older than Cyrus and had been with the Twelfth Maine Volunteers in Louisiana for a year. The vice president, however, had no qualms about his choice. He wrote to Coburn: [5]

I regret that arrangements had been made for the Cols of the colored regiments. I learn that Capt Bangs is an excellent officer and it certainly would have given me pleasure to aid him. I requested the apt of Appleton, for he merited it. My son was selected without my request or knowledge. I have seen him since and suggested to him to give the command to Capt B. He is unwilling now to do so after he had been selected by Genl Ullmann. Hence I cannot change the arrangement.

Probably in deference to Vice President Hamlin, who took a deep interest in Ullmann's project, Ullmann allotted two regiments to Maine, one to be commanded by Appleton and the other by Cyrus. On February 11, Cyrus received orders to report to Ullmann in New York. He was mustered in the next day as colonel of the Third United States Volunteers, although he did not receive his commission until the regiment was organized later in the year. A fragment of a letter reporting his arrival in New York survives, along with a letter to Coburn concerning Cyrus's selection of officers (mistakenly dated 1862)[6] and another short letter to Hannibal Hamlin.

New York Feb 12/63.

My Dear Father
    I arrived here all safe this morn. The names of McFaden & Sewell will go to Washington to day as Capts.
    I have received a letter from Mudgett & he is going with me—he asks that Charles Bridges of Castine—son of John Bridges—ordely sargent in his Co—be given a 1st Lt position & I have done it— I also give Carter & Moore of the 18th the posistions they desired—detachment for all of these will go to them immediatly—I have written to McFaden, Sewell & Henry Albert to report here with in ten days—

Your obt son
Cyrus Hamlin
    P.S. Tell Mr. Butler to send my Chaplin along within that time
C.H.

New York City Feb 16. 1862.
No 200 Broadway

Hon Abner Coburn
Gov of Maine
Dear Sir
    Application was made to me to take a Col. Ship of a Colord Regiment. I was desireous that some other person from our State should have it, but Gen Ullmann being desirous that I should go with him assigned two Reg^{t}s to the State of Maine, because I could not geet leave of absence to take any other possition = see General Order of War Dpt = Having obtained my leave of absence I intended to have started for maine to consult with you concerning the line officers but received orders to report to Genl Ullmann as a Mustering Officer I have been detained here & shall not be able to go to Maine at all The Sec of War gave me authority to select ten from the Army now in the field for my Officers I have selected

Willam S. Mudgett Captin 2.^{d} me for Lt Col
William A. Hatch Captin 3^{d} me for Maj
Orin McFaden of Woolwitch me – for Capt
C. W. Sewell of Foxcroft   "   "   "
J. H. Plaisted of 3^{d} Me   –   for 1st Lt
William S. Carter of 18th Me   "   "   "
Charles Bridges   " 2^{d} "   "   "   "
Joseph Hatch   " 20th "   " 2^{d} "
J. More   " 18   "   "   "   "
B Boggs _____ 2^{d} Lt

These men have been selected by the advice of my Father, Senator Morrill & Hon J. H Rice. Some of them I am acquainted with & are just the men I wish to have with me. Genl Ullmann has approved them & detachments, = those in the service = have gone to their Regs

I have promised the Chaplin's commission to a Methodist in Auburn Me. I desire that you will send me a good Surgeon as this is of the greatest importance. I have this day received the inclosed letters & as I have nominated a number of Line Offices I do not feel at liberty to add Websters name, not knowing what you have done. If you have a vacancy you may give him a 1st or 2^{d} Lt's possistion & assign him to my Reg. or Appletons

It is very important that you forward your lists as soon as possible as we desire to leave here in ten days In your list please to [grade] them. I have for Quartermas Sargent Henry Albert a colord man of Winterport who has seen eight years service in the English service.

Henry Farrer of Bangor who was raising a Cavelery Co. I learn did not succeed. If he would accept the Adj possiton I would like to name him—I have not communicated with him.

Hoping what I have done will meet with your approbation
I remaine

Your obt servt
Cyrus Hamlin
Capt. U.S.A.

New York Feb 19. 1863.
No 200 Broadway

My Dear Farther

I have concluded that you had better send me the money which you are to let me have by Express or send a check on New York by mail. If I draw on you at sight it will cost me as much as it would by Express to get it.

I do not see any p[r]ospect of our getting off any sooner than when you were here—we have not had a thing from Washington except a copy of my leave of absence

I have not heard from Orin McFaden of Woolwitch. I wish you would address him a note requesting him to come on at once.

Your obet son
Cyrus Hamlin

P.S. If you let Sis come on let me know when she will be here & by what port so I can meet here at the wharf—& in case I should not be there she can take a Hack & come to 238 Henry St Brooklyn.

C.H.

Governors played a key role in the appointment of not only the colonels of the Ullmann Brigade but the lower officers as well. Sometimes they had to satisfy other politicians, including Hannibal Hamlin (although, as we have seen, Governor Coburn resisted the selection of John Appleton as colonel).[7]

New York City Feb 24. 1863
No 200 Broadway

Hon Abner Coburn
Gov of Maine
Dear Sir
If this reaches you before you have forwarded the list of Officers for my Reg't you will confer a favor on my Father if you will give a 2^d Lt possition to James F. Merrill Co. D. 7th Regt Rhode Island, he is from Alfred Maine The delay has been caused by Father sending to him for recommendations & they did not reach me until this date.

Your obet servt
Cyrus Hamlin

As the other officers gradually arrived, Cyrus mustered them in. Bangs, who joined the Ullmann Brigade as lieutenant colonel of Appleton's regiment, later described Cyrus at this time as "an officer of fine executive ability, thoroughly conversant with 'rules and orders' from his association with Regular Army officers and heads of departments at Washington. He thus became our mentor in 'red tape' and our friend."[8]

Brooklyn March 8th 1863.

My Dear Father.
I have not written you since Sis came as she has informed you of her safe arrival.
I was unable to get mustered myself, while I could musters others & wrote to Senator Morrill & he got an order for Col Reeve to muster me, so I was mustered as of the 12 of Feb. (the date of my leave of absence) & am the ranking Col.
The men begin to arrive slowly but we expect to get off the last of this week. I shall keep Sis here until I go.
I inclose my note for two hundred dollars.
I saw Mrs Fremont & she said they have given the Genl plenty of promises, he is now in Washington

Marshall P. Getchell will be my adj. J. H. Plaisted will be my q.m. they are both from Waterville & have had experiance in these positions My Regt is the 3rd U.S. Volunteers Appletons 4th Col Botsford 1st of N.Y. Col Thomas 2nd which is the Mass Regt. Thomas is a Capt in the 10th Infantry & is from Portland, son of Major Thomas he is highly recommended by Gov Andrew. Love to all

Your obet son
Cyrus Hamlin

As the time for departing for New Orleans approached, Cyrus grew anxious about his personal safety, his new wife's security, and the reception his brigade would receive from General Banks, who had replaced Butler in the Department of the Gulf. Butler had been an efficient administrator who had cleaned up New Orleans physically, sternly suppressed flagrantly disloyal activities, and championed the cause of the black fighting man—all of which had naturally antagonized the civilians in and around the city. Lincoln hoped the less radical Banks would strengthen Unionist sentiment in Louisiana.

New York City March 26. 1863.
No 200 Broadway.

My Dear Father.

As Sarah has written you at home, often, since she has been here I have not ans your letters

We are still delayed here. Genl Ullmann went to Washington Sunday & expected to get back yesterday but has not returned. he went to get deffinate instructions about who, & when we may enlist men when we get to New Orleans so that we may not meet with opposistion from Genl Banks There are yet some twenty men yet to report the Genl took a man with him, which he will send directly to their Regt's with orders from the War Dept. so that they will all be here in a few days. We all expected to have been off before this but the War Dept. have delayed us so that we are not to blame There was a vacancy of a 1st Lt in my Regt & I have given to J. G. Hamlin (The Genl took his name to Washington)

I joined the Free Masons last week & I trust it will be a benefit to me should I ever be so unfortunate as to fall into the hands of the Rebels[9]

I have also had my life Insured for one thousand dollars for the benefit of my wife The policy I shall send to you. There is some mistake about the rate as the Agent told me it was only thirty six dollars a year but I understand it is about eighty, if so I may revoke it because I may not have the money to spare at that price for I desire to pay it in advance for a year

I enclose you a stamp for my note I did not think of it at the time I sent it.

We shall probably get off certainly by the last of next week. I presume by a Steamer to our-selves as there are quite two hundred of us & many take their horses from here.

Carmick was in to see me & says if Chase will give the assurance to the acting Comptroller (Jones) he will go on & make up & award damages & close the matter up he desired me to write you I told him I did not think you would do any thing more (—for I did not know upon what terms you might be with Chase—) He said Whittlesey the day before he died went to the office & had the thing ready to sign on the day following—but he died that day. He also showed me a letter from young Whittlesey[10] stating the same & that his father's dying words were to have it settled & also a remark was made upon his diary of the same effect It is provoking at least to get it so near settled & then get it stoped If you feel at liberty to do any thing more I have no doubt it would help it th[r]ough, but you can judge best about it.

Love to all

your obet son
Cyrus Hamlin

On April 10, the officers of the Ullmann Brigade boarded the transport Matanzas *bound for New Orleans, where they would recruit their men from Louisiana's large black population. Three days out to sea, Ullmann polled his officers on their recommendations for a course of action should the* Matanzas *meet up with the Confederate raider* Alabama. *With eight guns and a seasoned multinational crew of 144 officers and men, the* Alabama *had been wreaking havoc on Northern shipping since the previous September. Ullmann wanted to be prepared for a chance encounter. One officer suggested running up a strange flag so that the* Matanzas *might get close enough to the* Alabama *to allow the Union men to board and take the rebel raider. Another recommended flight, an impractical idea in view of the* Alabama's *great speed. Cyrus was less daring.[11]*

On board the Steamer Matanzas
At sea April 13. 1863.

General

I have the honor to submit the following opinions "should we fall in with the C. S. Steamer Alabama."

I would advise a surrender with such conditions, as we might be able to obtaine.

If not able to obtaine any conditions, I would advise an un[con]ditional surrender

It seems to me to be a rash as well as foolish act to attempt to capture any "manawar" without proper impliments & especialy in boarding the "Alabama" She being the [*sic*] our superior, in munitions of war, & of their disposall, & in number of men, thus giving them a great advantage while acting on the defensive, besides there is no ruse that we could adopt which would place us along side of the "Alabama" in order to graple with her before she could blow us out of the water with one broad side of her guns I can but think but think [*sic*] it would be throwing away many valuable lives without the slightest hope of success

I have the honor General
Very respectfully
You obt servt
Cyrus Hamlin
Col of 3 Regt U.S.V.

As it turned out, the officers of the Ullmann Brigade enjoyed a pleasant, uneventful voyage down the coast to Key West and across the Gulf to New Orleans. Some of the men, including Cyrus, had brought their wives along, and Bangs latter recalled "the merry company which gathered at the captain's table daily for two weeks."[12] Reaching New Orleans late in the afternoon of April 20, Cyrus immediately dispatched a chatty letter to his father, describing an exotic land new to his northern eyes.

New Orlans April 20. 1863.

My dear Father

We arrived here this afternoon about five we have had a very plesant trip indeed I believe there could not have been a plesanter one for we have had plesant & calm weather all the time. We reached the mouth of the Miss River last night just in season to get over the bar before dark, the fog became thick soon after & we were obliged to come to an anchor. We left Key West Friday morn under the convoy of the De Soto. We were not allowed to go ashore there, the Genl & his Staff visited the Flag Ship & that was all the communication we had save the Capt[13] of our Ship went a shore & got some green Turtles, Since which we have had Turtle, soups Roasts &c. which are very good. Just as we were coming over the bar & Masters Mate boats crew came from the Guard Ship they were so drunk that the Genl had them put under arrest, & sent a communication to the Ship when an Officer came & took them off. I mention this because the Masters Mate said he would publish it in the New York papers. The Dept will be doing wrong if they do not dismiss him from the service. I can not say that I am much pleased with the Miss River, the water is very high & most of the way up the river is higher than the land, but the Levee's keep it back. the water is of a yellowish mudy tint but after a while it settles & then it looks milky. We have been drinking it today & it is better than the water we have had from condensed steam We have passed many Plantations & probably the best in this State, we saw the hands to work upon the cane which is some foot & a half high, we also saw many orange groves, some few trees with the oranges yet upon them, although I learn the season for them is about Christmass, we saw roses in bloom, also the magnolia both white & red which grow as high as ten or fifteen feet, I saw some live oak trees, the first I have ever seen growing, they are very fine & look some like our elm but not so tall. The water cactus seems very plenty. The Plantations which we passed all looked very picturesque the Houses of the owners many like our New England homes while on either side to the right or left the negro quarters with a Street before them, they look much superior to those I have ever seen in Va. The Genl has gone on shore to night & left me in Com^d so I have not seen any of the city save what we saw sailing up. We are to have leave for all tomorrow when we shall go around it— The weather is like our June, & as yet I have not suffered any from it The nights are cool from the very heavy dew which commences to fall as soon as the sun sets & we have to dress warmer to keep from catching cold. As I have to go forward I will close to night & will try tomorrow, we expect to leave here in a day or two for Barton Rouge, we have to coal & get some arms first however here.

Your obet son

Cyrus Hamlin

In their efforts to recruit black soldiers, Ullmann and his officers ran into stiff competition from Banks. Although Banks had no use for black officers and pressured those he had inherited from Butler to resign,[14] he continued to raise troops for black regiments. Banks already disliked Ullmann, who had served under him in Virginia, and as commander of

the Department he viewed Ullmann as an interloper.[15] *Less than two
weeks after Ullmann arrived, Banks announced "the organization of a*
corps d'armée *of colored troops, to be designated as the* Corps d'Afrique."*[16] Although the order did not specifically state that the new organization would incorporate the Ullmann Brigade, that was Banks's obvious
intention.*

*In the meantime, the officers of the brigade set about recruiting their
regiments. Those of the First, Second, and Fourth Regiments proceeded
to the area around Brashear, southwest of New Orleans, which, as Bangs
observed, provided "an abundance of good material . . . for soldiers."*[17]
*Cyrus went to brigade headquarters at Baton Rouge, then garrisoned by
two regiments of the Louisiana Native Guards. Here he began to recruit
from runaway slaves seeking freedom behind Union lines, a practice sure
to increase the friction between Banks and Ullmann. On May 4, he sent
Captain William Nye twenty miles downriver to Plaquemine, where Nye
rounded up a company and one hundred women and children. Cyrus
described the events in a letter to his stepmother.*

*This letter to Ellen Emery Hamlin also contains wide-eyed descrip-
tions by Cyrus of the blacks with whom he was getting acquainted. In
Maine, which had a miniscule African American population, he might not
have known any blacks. The minstrel shows mentioned in the letter, with
their caricatures of black people and culture, perhaps shaped his image
of them. In Louisiana, Cyrus was learning first-hand about their ability
and willingness to learn, their love of family, and their culture (although
he seems to have missed the religious nature of the ring shout dance, an
Africanized Christian expression of spirituality). He was also discovering
the pervasive prejudice his men would face from white officers.*

Barton Rouge La. May 11th 1863.

My Dear Mother.

We have been here eleven days, the third after arriving here we left
the Steamer & the Genl was ordered to report to Genl Banks in person
over in the "Teche" country He sent the day before the 1st Regt Col Botsford & 2[d] Col Thomas over in that part of the county. I learned to night
through the 3 Regt native guards that they have all of their men—a company of that Regt went with them to do guard duty &c) The 4th Regt.
accompanied the Genl down river (I hear they have gone to Donaldsonville) Col Appleton has not reported—I opened a letter from him to the
Genl, he said Col Kimball said he would not permit a man of his to go
into a negro Regt if he could help it. & would not give him a furlough for
fear we might get him.— I was left here in command of two Regts & this
being Heiad [*sic*] quarters I have been quite busy. The first day we were

on shore the Ill Cavelery came in—you have before this read the account of their raid.[18] I think it is the greatest thing of the kind during the war— they brought in over a hundred colord men & we got such as were suitable for us. Maj Genl Auguer is in command here & is unfriendly to us. I went to him to obtaine permission to make a raid in the Country with the Cavelery & he would not let us, neither are we permitted to go out beyond the lines therefore we have to wait for those who come in & just now it is slow work. He told me that he could not allow us to go onto Plantations to enlist men on account of Genl Banks order. I have reported all of these things to Genl Ullmann who is now in New Orleans & he may order us a way now that we have just got settled. We have in both Regts here some three hundred men I sent Capt William Nye down to Plaquimine some twenty miles down the river on the 4th inst & he came back with a company bringing also about a hundred women & children. The Provost Marshall there done all the [*sic*] could to prevent his getting them but he told him he was an old Democrat and all of the men enlisted voluntarily & he would die for them before one of them should be returned to Slavery if they did not wish to go back. he took with him a smart colord private from one of the Regt here (there are three here 1[st] Col Safford—the line Officers are all black—3[rd] Col Nelson 4[th] Col Drew) who forme[r]ly lived there but ran a way, Capt Nye would let him when drilling the men march them back & past his old masters house until he could not stand it any longer & ask Capt Nye to have it stop— which he did not but kept on. The Planters who owned the men tried every way upon the men & him to get them back but it was no go. Capt Nye has been busy all day & has got the women & children comfortable places in the contraband camp, they would not let him leave the women & children there. My Regt is encamped the fartherest out of Town. We have a little cottage with three rooms, one we use as a kitchen one as a dinning room & the other as a sleeping room, the Hall which faces the road I use as my office My Regt is encamped on the side facing the City, the officers tents are in the yard. The Lt Col & Maj mess with us. I have to day succeeded in getting a good cook, his wife was a field hand & does the washing. I have a very nice little girl about fifteen who does the waiting. I want Sarah to take her north with her but she thinks we can not afford it. She has allways taken care of children, & is just the girl for you, if you would like her I will send her home by Sarah for you. I think you better take her, for she is just what you want. Her folks are willing she shall go north.[19] If you could see what I have seen you would believe that their affections are as strong as ours for those that are dear to them. We have for furniture a half dozen chairs, one table, a beadsted and mattress, 4 army bla[n]kets, a wash stand, with this we make out to keep house & get along nicely. We do not live as well as I could wish, for everything is very high except what we get of the commissary & that is not the nicest. To day I purchased for a dollar almost two qts of strawberries which were very good. We have green peas & beans & new potatoes. Milk which we get now & then we have to pay twenty cts per qt. Eggs are seventy cts per dozen. Butter is forty cts per lb. I got me a horse to day gave eighty dollars for him. he is black, just about such a horse as Jessie. You should be here & see one of the Plantation dances they make a ring & the dancers go in side, the others strike up & sing & clap their hands, before they get through the most of them usualy get a dancing. it is better than any thing I ever saw in any minstrel band. The Cavelery Regt Lt Col Zoulasky is encamped between me & the city, the other Eve our men had what they called a skirmish with them they met half way & seized them & brought them into camp & then paroled them by making them swear that they would not again fight against Infantry. they are up to these sort of things if we do not keep them busy. It is the universall opinion of all that they learn to d[r]ill much quicker than white men. & they never get to much of it, they have been found a[t] four O clock (we have rool call at 6½ O clock) in the morn, out drilling under some one of their own squad. then they are very obedient & do just what you ask them to do & not a word of complaint or growling is heard, but they prefer to drill than any thing else. When they are enrolled they are sworn upon the Bible, they most all understand the nature of an oath the officer who does it allways explains it to them. When they come to "obey the orders of the President" &c. they say "yes" they know that is, its "Abe Lincoln" I think we have not had a man but who knew who was the President. The best drilled troops at this Post are the Colored troops so conceeded by the officers I have not talked with an Officer but who conceeds it. I have not seen them except in a Dress Parade which was done in as good time & as well as I ever saw in my life. The Colord Officers of the 1st Regt are well educated men & some of them wealthy. the Col offers a thousand dollars to any Regt in this Dept of white officers if they can pass a better examination before a military board for military education & deportment as officers (some of them a[re] quite white & one or two of them are very black one of them in particular Capt Kio who came from St. Dimingo.) Yesterday 25 colord Rebel Soldiers were taken just out side of our lines I did not see them, but the Officer of the day told some of my Officers of it as he passed by here. it fails to ask the question whether they use them or not. When I first got here I called on Capt Frank Godfrey (John E. G-s son) he is in the Cavelery & is considered by all & very fine Officer, the best they have here, he is a brave & dashing officer, & they fear him greatly.

I have seen but one man (Lt Hill editor of the "Era" Genl Banks organ at New Orleans) but thinks that Butler was & is the man for this Dept.

the Sold[i]ers are disgusted with his [Banks's] milk & water policy, they say there is as much seditious language used in New Orleans as when the Rebels held the place, & in one church which Butler shut up because they would not pray for the President Banks allows it to go on & allows them to omit it. I send a Photograph home of a colord man who was whipped before last Christmas.

We have not heard from home yet but hope before long to get some letters. I will write Sis next Sarah joins in love to all. If we are situated as we are now I shall not let Sarah go home.

Your affect son
Cyrus Hamlin

P.S. Direct letters to me Genl Ullmanns Brigade New Orleans I want you to send me some Maine papers.

C.H.

At about this time, Cyrus heard with alarm the details of Banks's plans for the colored troops, including the limitation of the regiments to five hundred men instead of the usual one thousand, and he foresaw problems of organization and rank if Ullmann's brigade were to be included in the new Corps d'Afrique.[20]

unofficial   Barton Rouge May 12. 1863.

Genl Daniel Ullmann
Dear Sir,

Lt Hapgood called on me & left the recommendation of Col Dudley which I inclose to you. I am pleased with his appearance & should think him an energetic young man.

I see that Genl Banks has issued some Orders about raising some more Colord troops. I trust we are not included in that organization as I much prefer remaining as we were. I do not see why they are not to be the usual number, for there is any amount of material & this can be no reason for it. I can not see why or how it is more difficult to command one thousand men in this peculiar service with the proper officers, than any other, for the ratio of officers in a Regt of five hundred must be proportionate with that of a thousand. It strikes me that it will tend rather to make them more inefficient than effective If we are included in this peculiar organization how are we to be divided[?] Is the maj to have command of one Regt & the Lt Col the other? This will not do for their rank should be the same. Are the companies to be cut down to fifty men? & then retaine all of the officers upon the same footing as they are now? I look upon this as saying to men that are able & have the ability to command eighty two privates in white Regt, you are incompetent to command more than fifty colord men. I think-it would be far better if there is to be a change in organizing the Armies of this Country that the rank & file should rather be increased than decreased, after having obtained good & efficient officers.

The question of what we are to pay the men we are enlisting is frequently asked me. I have not been able to answer it. I hear that Col Nelsons men are paid the same as all Volunteers & I see no reason why our men should not have the same pay as all white Volunteers as we were organized before the last act of Congress which pays them ten dollars per month! Will you please informe me? I have had one man "Watson Nye" repo[r]t since you left, he is to be a 2 Lt in my Regt. I desire to muster him in & in that case what am I to do with the Supernumerary one? Perhaps it might be well for you to settle the question what will be done with the rest of them? As I am expecting all of my officers every day from New York.

Since making a report to you Col Dudley has gone out upon a reconnaissance Col Zoulasky Capts Roberts & Cantell accompanied him as "acting aids" Col Dudley is with us in our movements while I fear Genl Auguer is rather opposed to us.

Lt Hapgood desired me to state to you that if you gave him power to raise a Company of Artillery he would be able to secure six pieces of artillery—the same as they have in his present Company—by the aid of Capt Holstead Genl Auguers asst adj. Capt Holstead is truly a friend to our movement & without his aid these native guards whould have died out.

Col Zoulasky learned there were number of Free Colord men in New Orleans who did not enlist in the Infantry because they desired to go into the cavelery I do not think I am authorized to allow him to send an officer to enlist them, you being there, without your consent. Therefore I have ordered Capt Ghyka to report to you with the request that he may be allowed to enlist all suitable men.

I am Genl

Very respectfully
Your obt sevt
Cyrus Hamlin

NOTES

1. The earliest published account is probably Howard Carroll. *Twelve Americans: Their Lives and Times* (New York: Harper. 1883), 159-61. Hamlin's grandson published a version in his biography of Hannibal Hamlin in 1899, and I.

S. Bangs related the story as he had heard it directly from Hamlin. Charles Eugene Hamlin, *The Life and Times of Hannibal Hamlin* (1899: repr., Port Washington, N.Y.: Kennikat Press, 1971), 2:430-33; I. S. Bangs to Charles Hamlin, 4 March 1897, HFP; I. S. Bangs, "The Ullman [*sic*] Brigade," in *War Papers Read Before the Commandery of the State of Maine, Military Order of the Loyal Legion of the United States*, 2 (Portland, Maine: Lefavor-Tower, 1902): 290-92. See also H. Draper Hunt, *Hamlin: Lincoln's First Vice President* (Syracuse: Syracuse University Press, 1969), 163; Mark Scroggins, *Hannibal: The Life of Abraham Lincoln's First Vice President* (Lanham, Md.: University Press of America, 1994), 193-94. The story also found its way into fiction. Honoré Willsie Morrow, *With Malice Toward None* (New York: Morrow, 1928), 49-52. Ullmann himself stated that he and Hannibal Hamlin, carrying a note from Lincoln, visited Secretary of War Edwin M. Stanton on January 12, 1863, to discuss the question of black soldiers. Ullmann received his appointment the next day. Dudley Taylor Cornish, *The Sable Arm: Black Troops in the Union Army, 1861-1865* (1956; repr., Lawrence, Kan.: University Press of Kansas, 1987), 100-01.

2. John Appleton to William Pitt Fessenden, August 22, 1862, William Pitt Fessenden Papers, Western Reserve Historical Society, Cleveland; Israel Washburn, Jr., to John A. Andrew, May 24, 1862, John A. Andrew Papers, Massachusetts Historical Society, Boston.

3. Quoted in David M. Gold, "Frustrated Glory: John Francis Appleton and Black Soldiers in the Civil War," *Maine Historical Society Quarterly*, 31 (Summer 1991): 183.

4. Keith Wilson, "In the Shadow of John Brown: The Military Service of Colonels Thomas Higginson, James Montgomery, and Robert Shaw in the Department of the South," in *Black Soldiers in Blue: African American Troops in the Civil War Era*, ed. John David Smith (Chapel Hill: University of North Carolina Press, 2002), 307-09; Daniel Ullmann, *Address of Daniel Ullmann, L. L. D., before the Soldier's and Sailor's Union of the State of New York on the Organization of Colored Troops and the Regeneration of the South* (Washington, D. C.: Great Republic Office, 1868), 3.

5. Hannibal Hamlin to Abner Coburn, February (date unclear) 1863, formerly located in Civil War Correspondence—Governor, vol. 49, p. 180, Maine State Archives, Augusta (now untraceable following a reorganization of the archives).

6. Cyrus Hamlin to Abner Coburn, February 16, 1863, Maine Adjutant General Records, War Department Correspondence, Box 117, Folder 1, Maine State Archives, Augusta.

7. Cyrus Hamlin to Abner Coburn, February 24, 1863, Civil War Name File (Cyrus Hamlin), Box 119, Maine State Archives, Augusta (asking for an appointment of an individual as a favor to Hannibal Hamlin).

8. Bangs, "Ullman Brigade," 294.

9. As members of the same fraternity, freemasons were supposed to assist one another, even if they were on opposite sides in a war. For the story of a Union captain who claimed to have been saved by his membership in the order, and who reported meeting seven other Union officers whose lives had been similarly

spared, see Edward S. Ellis, *Low Twelve.* *"By Their Deeds Ye Shall Know Them."* *A Series of Striking and Truthful Incidents Illustrative of the Fidelity of Free Masons to One Another in Times of Distress and Danger* (New York: F. R. Niglutch, 1907), 148-66.

10. Elisha Whittlesey had six surviving sons at the time of his death.

11. Cyrus Hamlin to Daniel Ullmann, April 13, 1863, Records of the Adjutant General's Office, 1780's-1917, General's Papers, Daniel Ullmann, Record Group 94, National Archives and Records Administration, Washington, D.C.

12. Bangs, "Ullman Brigade," 297.

13. The *De Soto* was commanded by Captain William M. Walker. *OR*, ser. 1, vol. 17, p. 418.

14. James G. Hollandsworth, Jr., *Pretense of Glory: The Life of General Nathaniel P. Banks* (Baton Rouge: Louisiana State University Press, 1998), 148-49.

15. Ibid., 151-52.

16. *OR*, ser. 1, vol. 15, pp. 716-17.

17. Bangs, "Ullman Brigade," 306.

18. From April 17 through May 2, 1863, Colonel Benjamin Grierson led the Sixth and Seventh Illinois Cavalry Regiments on a devastating raid through Confederate territory, ending up at Baton Rouge. Stephen Z. Starr, *The Union Cavalry in the Civil War*, vol. 3, *The War in the West, 1861-1865* (Baton Rouge: Louisiana State University Press, 1985), 187-95.

19. Domestic service in the homes of the growing Northern middle class was one of the few occupations open to recently freed young black women. After the war, the Freedmen's Bureau sent many black girls and young women to service jobs in the North. Faye E. Dudden, *Serving Women: Household Service in Nineteenth-Century America* (Middletown, Conn.: Wesleyan University Press, 1983), 222-26.

20. Cyrus Hamlin to Daniel Ullmann, May 12, 1863, Records of the Adjutant General's Office, 1780's-1917, General's Papers, Daniel Ullmann, Record Group 94, National Archives and Records Administration, Washington, D.C.

Chapter Five

Banks and the Corps d'Afrique

By the end of May, Banks had learned first-hand of the fighting ability of black troops. He was conducting a campaign against the Confederate fortress at Port Hudson on the Mississippi River. On May 27, the Louisiana Native Guards displayed conspicuous courage during a general assault on the fort. Nevertheless, Banks brought the Ullmann Brigade more directly under his control, with what seems in retrospect to be an intention to keep it out of action. On June 6, Banks's Order No. 47 renamed the First through Fifth regiments of the brigade the Sixth through Tenth regiments of the Corps d'Afrique. (The Louisiana Native Guards also became part of the Corps.) Ullmann accused Banks of toadying to the local planters. "Gen. Banks talks and writes very well on this question of arming blacks," he wrote to Hannibal Hamlin, "but his action comes limping in the rear at a vast distance. He is striving too much to make friends among these planters, whose loyalty is a simple farce." From the time Banks first proposed the new organization, recalled Bangs, "Practically, we were never under [Ullmann's] orders."[1]

In the midst of these frustrations and disappointments with the brigade, Cyrus suffered a personal tragedy: the death of his young bride.

New Orleans July 17. 1863

My Dear Father

It is with sorrow & mourning that I sit down to informe you of the death of my Dear Wife. On the fourth she was not quite well but seemed to be cold, she had taken cold, & it had prevented her menstrating, on the 5th she was well & in good spirits so much so that she wrote a little to her Mother after tea. On Monday did not feel quite well & when she went to bed took a mustard foot bath & on Tuesday morning she got up & went to the window & took cold again. I called the Dr then & we gave her a sweat & she commenced to menstate & felt nicely she was confined to her bed but was getting a long nicely. she seemed about the same Wednesday Thursday & Friday, but Saturday her flowing stoped, she was nervous & tired for the want of sleep. I was somewhat frightened & sent for the Medical Director Dr Van Nostrum he brought with him Dr

Rice of Mass and Dr Ratborn of the Navy. they said there was no danger
whatever & rather laughed at me. They advised morphia to be given her
& on the next morn she would be well 5/8 of a grain was given her &
from eleven O clock that night until about eight o clock Sunday she slept
nicely & said she was almost well I talked with her some time & thought
she would get tired out talking, so I told her so & advised her to sleep. I
waked her up about ten & she was the same but about twelve I tried to
wake her & had hard work to do so. I again sent for the Medical Director
& the same gentlemen came. It was then they told me she could not live
& on that day Sunday Eve at ten minutes past seven she died. She was
not concious when she expired but died very easy & seemed to know
nothing about it, the last words she spoke was just before the Medical
Director came she wanted to get up & I held her up when she put her
arms around me & said "kiss me, after which she said lay me down for I
am fainting. I have her body [here] & have it preserved & am coming
home with it in the first [Gov] Transport, which is expected every moment to arrive & will leave here in three days after it. Capt Mudgett ac-
companis me. Father go to her Mother & tell her of it. She blames me for
allowing her to come with me at all but I could not refuse to have her
with me when she wanted to come & I wanted her to. I feel as if I had
lost all that is left & that I now have nothing to live for I try to think it
may be right in Gods way & endure it as best I can but Father it is very
hard to loose her that was so dear. I will Telegraph you when I reach
New York City when I will be in Bangor Make ne[ce]ssary arrangements
for her [burial] it is time for the mail to close & they are waiting for this,
& I have not the heart to write more

Your aff son
Cyrus Hamlin

*Cyrus obtained leave to bring Sarah's body back to Maine. Bangor
attorney John Edwards Godfrey noted in his journal entry for August 2
that Cyrus had "returned to New York from New Orleans with his dead
wife, whom he carried out there a bride a short time ago." On August 13,
Cyrus was in Bangor on an extended furlough. The trip home saved him
from a confrontation with Brigadier General Godfrey Weitzel, about
whose attitude toward black troops he had made some indiscreet remarks.
Personal tragedy could not overshadow concerns about the war for long.
Cyrus was soon in Washington visiting his father. On August 22, Hanni-
bal Hamlin addressed a note to Lincoln "to be handed to you by my son
Cyrus," who had come to the capital "to submit to you and the Secy of
War the difficulties and embarrassments under which the [Ullmann]
Brig[ade] has suffered."[2]*

*Cyrus returned to Louisiana on September 11, possibly without hav-
ing presented his complaints to the president. (Lincoln wrote to the vice
president that very day that he had not heard from Cyrus.³) The "difficulties and embarrassments" continued. Cyrus's under-strength regiment,
finally organized that month at Port Hudson, belonged to the Second
Brigade, First Division, Corps d'Afrique. At the end of October he found
himself in command of the Second Brigade. A week later he inspected the
four regiments in his charge and found his black troops sadly neglected
by the army. The inspection report is in Cyrus's name, but not in his
handwriting.⁴*

Head-Quarters 2ⁿᵈ Brigade
1ˢᵗ Division Corps d'Afrique
Port Hudson November 6 1863

To Captain R. Des Anges
Acting Ass't Adj't General
Head-Quarters 1ˢᵗ Division Corps 'd.Afrique
Sir,

In compliance with Special Order N° 9 dated Head-Quarters, 1ˢᵗ Division, Corps 'd.Afrique, I have the honor of submitting the following
report as the result of the Monthly Inspection of this Brigade which took
place on Sunday 1ˢᵗ Ultimo.

The Troops presented a fair military appearance.

Arms. Kept clean but with the exception of the 7ᵗʰ & 9ᵗʰ Regiments are of
poor quality being the old fashioned altered flint lock. Smooth bore.

Clothing. Fair condition, generally good.

Equipments. In a fair condition.

Accoutrements. In good order, nicely blacked & brasses polished.

Kitchens. In good order. convenient and well kept.

Guard Houses. Fair but too open for inclement weather.

Regimental and Company books are neatly and well kept but a deficiency
exists for which requisition will be made.

Transportation. Inadequate.

Camp Equipage. Not complete. many of the Tents are badly mildewed,
having been in use by the 9 months Regiments before being issued.

To place the Brigade in a thoroughly effective condition for service I
would respectfully recommend the necessity of exchanging the arms of
the 8ᵗʰ & 10ᵗʰ Regiments for a superior kind of weapon for although the
arms at present in possession of the companies are serviceable, yet the
majority of them being old altered muskets they are very liable to be put
out of order. I would urge the importance of providing the Brigade with
Armorers and Arm tool chests.

In view of the present rainy season it is absolutely necessary that India Rubber Blankets should be issued to the men immediately.

The lack of large sized shoes is also a subject of continual complaint and inconvenience, and steps should be taken for obviating the evil.

Some measures ought to be adopted for supplying the Soldiers with anti-scorbutic food, several cases of scurvy having occurred in consequence of the almost total absence of all vegetable food from the men's rations.

3 waggons and 7 mules are required to complete the means of Transportation.

I am

Very Respectfully
Your Obedient Servant
Cyrus Hamlin
Colonel Com^{dg}

Whether because of the treatment received by his troops, the tedium of garrison duty at Port Hudson, plain ambition, or some combination of the three, Cyrus informed his father of his intention to resign from the Corps d'Afrique. His resolve seems to have fluctuated along with his opinion of Brigadier General George L. Andrews, in charge of the District of Port Hudson, and Andrews' promotion policy.

Port Hudson Nov 8. 1863.

My Dear Father

Your letter of the 19th was received & burnt as requested.

When I arrived here I found some illfeeling because Col Clark had been mustered back, so that he ranked Col Appleton, therefore took command of the Brigade—I supposed Col Appleton had fully explained the matter to you ere this—which is a great injustice & I hope it will be rectified. Many of the Officers—those whome I told that I was about to leave the service desired that I would not do it until Col A— returned. Genl Banks being away upon an expedition it was no use to send in my Resignation until he returnes therefore I have not sent my resignation in & will not until I hear from you I have had Command of the 2^d Brigade 1st Division—7, 8, 9 & 10 Regts—since I have been here, until yesterday I took command of the Division, Genl Ullmann com^{ds} the the [*sic*] co[r]ps Genl Andrew being away. I am senior Col of the Corps & shall try & get recommended for a Brig Genl. Every one here heard & some one said they had seen me while at the North with a Star The officers of the Brigade are desirous that it may be done & will do all they can for me.

I have been studying upon the movements of a Brigade & there are but a few but what I am thoroughly acquainted with. So that I would not be afraid to take it out upon any occasion & put it in any possition or through any evolution that is generaly used

We are doing nothing but fatigue work, rebuilding & strength[en]ing the outer works & building a new line of interior works, which makes it very hard for the men for they are on fatigue one day & the next on guard duty the only cessation they have is Saturday P.M. & Sunday, so they get no drill what ever, but I hope in a few weeks we will get through fatigue work. The troops here are all colord except three Batteries & one Regt of Heavy artillery & a Cavelery Regt. Last Sunday Genl Ullmann reviewed my Brigade & I inspected it. I get home sick sometimes wish I out of here but am getting use to it

I wish you may use your influence if Brig Genl Dwight is recommended for a Maj Genl, to get it, not confirmed for he is a drunken & disgracefull man & ought to be dissmissed the service[5] I hear the reason Genl Banks did not make a move was because he (Banks) owes his Father borrowed money I will try & get some orders he issued & send them to you which will show for themselves He villified us in his report & when Genl Ullmann asked for an investigation Genl Banks says he better let the thing drop as Dwight belongs to a very wealthy & one of the first families in Mass. Genl Andrews I like very much & is really doing the right thing & is very strict, has a school of the officers himself so that the drill shall be uniform in the Corps,[6] putting him at the head instead of Ullmann is a change for the better. I did not think so when I was at home. I very much wish you will see the Sec of War personally & have our Commissions sent to us, it may be a small thing but the Officers are very anxious & care a great deal about it. it ought to have been done long ago but the pressure of business at the Dept has delayed it but if you will call the matter up they will be forthwith coming.

Love to all

Your obet son
Cyrus Hamlin

Direct
2 Brigade 1st Division Corps d'Afrique
Port Hudson via New Orleans

Hd Qts 2 Brigade 1st Division
Corps d Afrique Port Hudson
December 10. 1863.

My Dear Father

I have just finished writing to Senator Morrill & Hon Mr Rice asking them to use their influence to have me promoted to Brigadier General. I have spoken plainly that they may know why I ask it. Genl Andrews has asked that one Lt Col Fisk 2nd La (white) Vol Infty may be appointed Brg Genl. The Officers of the 1st Brigade have come to me & say they [*sic*] as Genl Andrews has established the rule that promotion shall be by seniority they do not consent that any promotions shall be made outside of the Corps of a lower rank to superceed us. Col Fisk is not a superior officer but a pet of Andrews he is one of those who was opposed to us when we came out & now after suffering what we have, insults on one side & obstacles on the other to have such men who have tried to crush us put over us is an injustice which I with [others] am not willing to submit to. They come to me & told me if I would work for myself they would do all in their power to help me & I being the senior [Col] am entitled to it. I judged from your letter that in all probability I would remaine here & in the service which being the case I can not after taking the possition at the time I did & fighting through what we have to do remaine calmly & let a man be placed over me when the only desire he has is promotion, submit to it especialy after he having done what he could to crush us & now when we have made a reputation & proved to the world what we *believed* is *true* have him placed over me. I am aware the rule you established when this administration came into power that you could not ask for any thing for us, it being a personal matter. This is a matter that effects others besides myself and in justice to this Corps I hope you may be able to help me either before the Sec of War or the President I have not done anything to gain a brilliant Victory but I have been compelled to suffer more than in fighting in standing by & aiding when the last hope has all but left us. I am entitled to it by rank & I ask in justice to us that we may have Officers whose heart & sympathy is with us for God knows we have to many now of the other kind. If the delegation see fit to recommend me I do not want you to stop them but rather have them do it, if you can not aid me before the Sec of War or the President let them do what they may be able to, for I deserve it & can fill the position. The position will be filled either from out side or here, out side if we do not prevent it. I am homesick at times & almost wish I was out of the service & many times have had a mind to resign I sent an appointment to War Dept for Sutler for my Regt I wish when you are at the War Dept you would call it up & have it confirmed by the Sec of War & send the Commission to me. Love to all

Your obet son

Cyrus Hamlin

Head Quarters 2^d Brigade

1st Division "Corps d Afrique"

Port Hudson Dec 26. 1863.

My Dear Father.

I received your letter of the 9th this day. I have been looking anxiously every mail to hear from you although I expected as yet you would not have had time to examine into those matters which have concerned me. I have almost given up the hope that I shall leave the service, but hope the future will develope that will either give me cause either to remain or to resign. the work we have to do is just but the way we are treated is shamefull & the only reason is that we were the first who came into this organization. they have & are doing all that can be done that our iden[t]ity may be lost & that we may be wholely forgotten. Genl Andrews after promoting such officers as he sees fit establishes the rule that it shall be by seniority but must first go before a board which they must pass an examination. I find no fault with this but officers of other Brigades are promoted by his option with out any regard to his rule When I call his attention to it am told I "have no right to comment upon the actions of the Comdg Genl" & says that if any officer tries to get promotion in this Corps except through him he will do every thing in his power to break him" It seems to me that an officer that talks thus has neither the judgement or wisdom to command a Regiment The officers and men of this Brigade number only 1755. this includes every thing. Genl Banks order allows us 500 to a Regiment which makes us about four hundred short. Why have we not been filled up. I can not tell for there has been an average of twenty officers on recruiting service form [*sic*] this Brigade & all they have recruited were given to other Regt's. Genl Thomas said while here Genl Banks had no right & that it was contrary to Law to raise 500 to a Regt. The Officers seem to think & I am inclined to believe it, that we will be consolidated, & that it will be a very plausable excuse to the Country to take our men & put them into these new Regts because they are full & it would not be right to put the greater with the less. therefore our office[r]s will be mustered out of service. Yet the influence that we possess at home may save us. Genl Andrews is unpopular with the whole command & I trust he may not be made a Maj Genl. I hope that you will succeed in getting justice done for Col Appleton. one point is that Col Clark had no right to be mustered at all under Genl Banks orders for at that time & has not now seven companies where is he should have

ten to entitle him to that position It also does great injustice to Lt Col
Zoulaski who has had a full Regt all the time & came out with us in
Com^d of his Regt Clark should not be permitted to rank even him. If they
wish any papers to be forwarded I can send them to you. The Officers of
this Brigade will be under great obligations to you if you can but secure
to them the Commissions which were promised to them I wish they
might be sent direct to Genl Ullmann & then we would be shure to get
them. It is feared that Andrews might withhold them if they fell into his
hands & have some of Genl Banks Provisional Commissions sent instead,
which we do not wish & I for one will not accept. The papers that I sent
to you was for you to read & to be used against Genl Dwight, for no sane
man would ever give such orders. While North he was kicked out of the
Fifth Avenue Hotel for having a New Orleans strumpet with him, his
conduct was the same on the Steamer coming out. Hon Mr Flanders
would not be introduced to him. he is a disgrace to any service a coward
& a villian. I want as I wrote you before not to do anything against me if
the delegation will recommend me for promotion. If they put any one
over me I shall resign for I can not have the spirit of a man to remain If
you could be here & see the posistion I occupy I think you would lend
your aid, for no one could then do more then I for the interest of the corps
for the rank would carry respect. all here look upon me, being the son of
the Vice President that I would have only to ask for a position or make it
known that I wished for it & it would be granted. it makes me feel very
bad some times that they look upon it in that light but such is the case. &
I ask you how I could stand the humiliation to have one placed over me
& by those who have no interest in our welfare but their own promotion,
either the position I took with other officers in this organization when it
was doubtful & the Country not believing in it, is worthy of some credit
or none, if it is, then being senior Col of all the Colord troops in this Dept
I am entitled to promotion, if you could hear the Officers not only of this
Brigade but in the others talk you could but come to the same conclusion,
it was at their earnest solisitation that caused me to start in the matter. the
office[r]s in or rather Col Dickey Comdg 1st Brig went before coming to
me & saw Genl Ullmann who told him (since me) that he would do any
thing any thing any thing [*sic*] in the world for me he saw Genl Banks &
he gave him to understand that he would recommend me. I do not place
any confidence in Banks for he is in the habit of making promises without fulfiling them, yet trying as he is to be President—which I pray he
never may be—he may think it agood stroke of policy. I would ask to be
left in Com^d of this Brigade were to get promotion for its history is to
strongly connected with me & they all look upon me as possessing that
influence that will carry them through all of our trials. they look upon it
as a right that the pioneers are entitled to this much & they ask this as

their right no one can say but that I have done my duty well & faithfull the Asst Inspector Genl told me I had the best Brigade in the Corps & yet we had not drilled so much as some of the others. I am at times very disconsolate, with the loss of my wife yet fresh & these other mental anxi[e]ties. I sometimes wish there might be a place where I might go & forget every one & every thing, life seems worth but little & when I strive to do what is good & to accomplish what I may I find but little consolation. I will close as I wish to write to Charlie & Sister

Your obj son

Cyrus Hamlin

Still complaining about Andrews more than two months later, Cyrus also showed a growing interest in Louisiana politics, concern over the machinations of "political" generals, and continued disgust at the treatment of his brigade. However, it is not clear what the personal matter was that he refers to in his letters of February 26 and March 13. It may have been his effort to get promoted.

Anxious to "reconstruct" Louisiana as a free state, President Lincoln urged Banks to organize a government as expeditiously as possible. On February 22, Banks ordered elections for state officers in which adult white males who took a loyalty oath could participate. Three Unionist candidates ran for governor. With Banks's support, moderate Michael Hahn defeated J. Q. A. Fellows, a conservative, and Benjamin F. Flanders, a supposed radical who during the campaign disavowed any notion of black equality.

Headquarters 2d Brigade. 1st Division, C. d' A.

Port Hudson, La., Feb 26 1864.

My dear Father.

I received a letter from Charlie upon his arrival at Bangor & about a fortnight since, one from Senator Morrill, in which they said my interests would be protected, & that you had written me fully about my matters. Your letter must have been lost as I have not received it. Will you write me again so that I may learn what is status of my matters. We are expecting Genl Thomas here every day who is to give us a very thorough Inspection. I am very sorry that I have not received your letter before he comes here. Genl Andrews I am quite confident fears me & I also fear him for I think if he dared he would place me where I would have only my Regt to Command these are only opinions & may be wrong as far as my duties go he finds no fault with me. I heard that he thinks Ullmann & I are trying to kill him off so that Ullmann will get Command of the

Corps. it is not so as we are both satisfied with our present Commands. although personaly I would like to see Ullmann there, for in him I have a good friend

The election has passed & Hahn is elected by about two thousand majority. I do not think there is much difference between him and Flanders in principle, except Banks controlles Hahn, & the whole strength of the Dept was used to elect him. Flanders would have been nominated if every thing had been done honorable but the Convention was broken up by Hahn's friends when they saw they were in the minority. I have no doubt but two Senators will be sent by Banks's choice.

I am sorry to say I learnd that Genl Banks is not a *pure* man in his private life[7]

Your obet son
Cyrus Hamlin

Cyrus's political interests reached beyond Louisiana. Secretary of the Treasury Salmon P. Chase, a politically ambitious, radically antislavery figure, had grown apart from Lincoln and was angling to replace him on the Republican ticket in the next presidential election. His maneuverings supposedly included negotiations with General Banks, a former Speaker of the House who harbored presidential ambitions of his own.

Headquarters 2d Brigade. 1st Division, C. d' A.
Port Hudson, La., March 13 1864.

My Dear Father.

I have been watching anxiou[s]ly every mail for a letter from you. I hope soon to learn what disposition has been done for my case. I have not heard from you since I sent you, some recommendations. Did you receive them? Or have they got lost, like your letters, if so, I will send some more. Genl Thomas has not been here yet, although we expect him every day. Has anything been done with Genl Butler's request, to have Col Appleton, ordered to him? Col Zoulavsky returned from the North Friday. he informs me that Genl Banks, has sold out to Chase. He is to give all his aid, real or imaginary chances, which he has for the nomination of President, in the coming Convention, & in return if Chase succeeds, Banks is to have an appointment abroad, for the next four years, after which Chase is to give his aid to him for the next nomination. I think you can place confidence in this, for it comes from Maj Plumbly, who is an intimate friend of Bank's,—who is to have Flanders place as Com[s] of Internal Revenue if Flanders can be induced to resign—& told

Zoulavsky of it. Collector Dennison of New Orleans, went to Washington, & made the negotiations with Chase, & Zoulavsky was present, in the house when Dennison returned & met Banks, & made known the result. It strikes me if Mr Lincoln desires to be renominated, his friends had better go to work or Chase will gain the day. What do you think of the chances of renomination? Judging from the press, Chase can not carry "New York", Banks & Sprague may be able to give him some aid in New England.

Genl Andrews will make a strong effort, to fill us up, when Genl Thomas comes, if that can not be done, he will have us consolidated, in order to do this, he will have some of us ordered before a board for examination.[8] in case he does this I shall get all the officers—which will be quite all in this Brigade—to send in as strong protest, as we are able to get up, & accompany it with our resignations. I do not fear an examination, but after what we have done, if we are to be treated in this way by eleventh hour men, I think the quicker we get out of this Dept the better it will be for us. Should I get my promotion, which I think *this Administration* in justice ought to give it to me, I think I might be able to prevent it, as I could then give my views & they would have some weight & be respected. Nothing new here. There is no force in this vicinity except a few Cavalry which can do nothing with us.

Love to all

Your Affectionate son
Cyrus Hamlin

P.S. Has Charlie got a position with Col Wentworth in his Regt. I think you ought to obtain it for him, if he has not.

Hd Qts 2 Brigade 1st Division CdA
Port Hudson April 1st 1864.

My Dear Father.

I have just received your letter of Jan 12th which explains my condition I, think as you there say, things had better remain as they are Genl Andrews has changed his mind from some cause or rather [*sic*] & will ask Genl T— to allow no promotions to be made out of our Corps, this is perfectly satisfactory to me. There was a rumor throughout the Post last week that I had received a Commission as Brig. Genl. it came from one of the Clerk's at Hd Qts who said he had recorded a com^s for me. I believe I have not written you that Genl Banks a few weeks since of his own accord promised Genl Ullmann again that he would recommend me. Genl Thomas has not been here yet, & and we do not know when he will be here, he is to organize this Corps or rather the Colord troops into a Corps so our name & numbers will be changed he has already commenced to number them in other parts of the Country. We probably shall be combined into one army Corps, the numbers commence numbering from the Regular Army. I have orders to prepare for the field, shall probably leave here in about ten days. I am to have men transfered from the 2nd Division which will give me an effective force of over twenty three hundred. Genl Banks is in the Teche Country pushing for Shreveport with parts the 13 & 19 Army Corps, three Brigades of 16 Army Corps & Genl Steels force from Arkansas. which makes a strong combination. I do not believe Banks cares for colored troops & only does for them what he is oblidged to do. I do not think he will give us any chance to advance with him. I hope to see Genl Thomas but may not. if you do not hear from it might be best to let matters remain as they are until just before Congress adjourns, but you can judge as to that better than I can. I like Genl Andrews better the more I become acquainted with him. We might go father & face worse.

Your affectionate son
Cyrus Hamlin

NOTES

1. I. S. Bangs. "The Ullman [*sic*] Brigade," in *War Papers Read Before the Commandery of the State of Maine, Military Order of the Loyal Legion of the United States*, 2 (Portland, Maine: Lefavor-Tower, 1902): 304. Bangs did not view the disregard of Ullmann as a bad thing. He thought Ullmann was utterly incompetent. Ibid., 297.

2. John Edwards Godfrey, *The Journals of John Edwards Godfrey, Bangor, Maine, 1863-1869* (Rockland, Me.: Courier-Gazette, 1979), 28; Cyrus Hamlin to Captain Moses C. Brown, August 13, 1863, Daniel Ullmann Papers, New-York Historical Society, New York; *Private and Official Correspondence of Gen. Benjamin F. Butler during the Period of the Civil War* (Norwood, Mass.: Plimpton Press, 1917), 3:103-04; Roy P. Basler, ed., *The Collected Works of Abraham Lincoln* (New Brunswick, N.J.: Rutgers University Press, 1953), 6:439-40.

3. Basler, *Collected Works of Lincoln*, 6:439.

4. Cyrus Hamlin to Robert Des Anges, November 6, 1863. Records of the Adjutant General's Office, 1780's-1917, General's Papers, Daniel Ullmann, Record Group 94, National Archives and Records Administration, Washington, D.C.

5. For a similar assessment of Dwight, see Edward Bacon, *Among the Cotton Thieves* (Detroit: Free Press Steam Book & Job Printing House, 1867), 158-61.

6. Although Andrews disliked the idea of black officers, he did not share Banks's more general prejudice against black soldiers. He also tried to improve the quality of his white officers. James G. Hollandsworth, Jr., *The Louisiana*

Native Guards: The Black Military Experience During the Civil War (Baton Rouge: Louisiana State University Press, 1995), 84-86.

7. Perhaps Cyrus had heard rumors of Banks's recently-conceived idea of using proceeds from the sale of confiscated cotton to bribe Confederate officers into quitting the war and concluded that Banks himself sought to profit from the scheme. Banks never implemented the plan, and while the Department of the Gulf was awash in corruption, there is no evidence of dishonesty on Banks's part. Fred Harvey Harrington, *Fighting Politician: Major General N. P. Banks* (Philadelphia: University of Pennsylvania Press, 1948), 135-38.

8. In May 1863, the War Department established boards of examination to try to ensure that black units received competent, upright officers. The New Orleans board was notoriously lax. Joseph T. Glatthaar, *Forged in Battle: The Civil War Alliance of Black Soldiers and White Officers* (New York: Free Press, 1990), 38, 52.

Cyrus Hamlin

Hannibal Hamlin

Sarah Emery Hamlin, Cyrus Hamlin's mother

CM Bee (signature)

WASHINGTON, D. C.

Ellen Emery Hamlin, Cyrus Hamlin's stepmother

Charles and Cyrus Hamlin

Major General John C. Frémont, Commander
of the Mountain Department in 1862

Major General Benjamin F. Butler, Commander
of the Department of the Gulf in 1862

Major General Nathaniel P. Banks, Commander
of the Department of the Gulf, 1862–1864

Brigadier General Daniel Ullmann, Commander
of the Ullmann Brigade

Chapter Six

In Command: Bonnet Carré and Port Hudson

On April 17, 1864, Ullmann, on behalf of Andrews, who was ill, sent Cyrus and the Eightieth U.S.C.T. to the District of Bonnet Carré, north of New Orleans.[1] There may have been sound military reasons for the transfer, or Andrews may have been attempting to placate Cyrus or just get him out of his hair. Whatever the reason, Cyrus seems to have been pleased by the change of scene. As the next several letters attest, however, he was thinking more and more about his post-war life.

Hd Qts 80 Regt U. S. Infrantry
Bonnet Carre April 24th 1864

My Dear Father.

Just a week ago orders were issued for my Regt to proceed to this place & relieve the 133rd N.Y. Regt. The (10th) 82nd Regt were ordered to Ft Barrancas Fla. the same time I joined my Regt & with four Companies reached here Wednesday. Maj Hatch with the rest of the Regt joined me here Friday. The 133rd have not left yet. they will go as soon as a Steamer can be obtained to take them. the boats are all busy carrying troops to the Red River. Since I last wrote you I have seen Genl Thomas, he was at Port Hudson a fortnight ago to day, & reviewed my Brig. he said he was "very much pleased with our appearance" & expressed the wish to soon to have us up to the front, but since then things are changed. Our names & numbers are changed now & instead of 8th I am now the 80th United States Infantry. From all I can learn we were badly whipped on the 8 & 9th above Alexandria since that time all the white troops in the Dept have & are being sent up. Officers who were there say that a Flag of truce was sent to Banks saying that if he put colord troops in to a fight they would not "give any quarter to any troops" if captured. I am inclined to believe this as the 1st Brig of our Div was sent to the rear & the rest of the Colord troops at Port Hudson are to be sent to relieve white troops, while they are to be sent to the front. I think Banks better retire to private life. This Post is thirty eight miles from New Orleans on the same side of the river.

The inhabitants are very bitter upon us I hear they have sent in a petition & say they will give forty thousand dollars for a Post fund if they will send us away. I do not believe any attention will be paid to it. The inhabitants are all Creoles—Slidells & Beauregards Father in law lives just above here The most of them have large plantations & are very rich. I do not expect they will show me any hospitality but I do not care for that, as I shall try & do my duty. I have twenty eight miles on the river to guard mostly to prevent smuggling. I shall have some Cavalery to patrool above as far as Donaldsonville. I am much pleased with the command if I am not to go to the front or if going am only to do fatigue work. This is a healthy place & after getting settled I shall like. I am now out side of the Post proper as this Regt are not friendly to us & I think it easier to keep out then get out after getting into trouble. Love to all.

Your obedt son
Cyrus Hamlin

P.S. Genl Thomas told Genl Ullmann that he should recommend me in his next letter to the President. Genl Ul— is in Command of the Port Hudson Genl Andrews has gone home very sick. Direct my letters to *New Orleans*

C.H.

Headquarters U. S. Post
Bonnet Carre May 4th 1864.

My Dear Father.

I was up the river on Sunday to my eighteen mile station & while there purchased some Perique tobbacco. I shall send you & Charlie a karat of it by express. This tobbacco is only made in this State—in the Parish of Ascension—it is superior to all other tobbacco. A leaf is rolled & cloth put round it. then it is wound with rope, when dry, another leaf is rolled round it & the same process pursued, until it has the desired size. It is sold in New Orleans at wholesale at two dollars & fifty cents per pound. In using it, it should be cut across the end. I do not hear anything from Red river, this Post being so near New Orleans Steamers do not touch. I do not as yet know much about this Country or the people I am now waiting for a Steamer to go to New Orleans to see Genl Reynolds. The only thing to be feared is that a few guerrillas may get th[r]ough the swamps & burn & destroy a plantation before we can get at them. I think is a great deal of smuggling carried on by small boats coming up the river under permits of the Internal Revenue. The crops are very backward as the weather has been so cold. Cotton is the only crop planted as they say it does not pay to go into the sugar business although it is selling for twenty three cts per [lb]. I had some strawberries & cream last Saturday,

I purchased on the same day some berries which resemble our blackber-
ries I do not recollect the name they have for them here. I will write
Charlie on my return I commenced a letter to him at Port Hudson but did
not have time to finish it. Love to all.

Your obst son
Cyrus Hamlin

P.S. Direct to me at Bonnet Carre Via New Orleans.

C.H.

Headquarters United Stats Post
Bonnet Carre June 5 1864.

My Dear Father.

I received your & Sisters letter of the 15 of May yesterday.

I have written Mr. Shirley to see Mr Stovers agent & to state to him
the circumstances concerning the ponies & to write you what their ans
was. I have not considered them mine for I wrote Stover that as they were
given to me on condition that I would go to New York I returned them as
I could not fullfil the condition If they consider that it belongs to me, I
wish you to pay the bill & take him away & put him out to pasture or
keep him in the Stable at home & charge the expenses to me. It might be
used for Hannie to learn to ride &c. I have been trying to save some
mony but my expenses while at home has kept me back I am square now.
I have sent a hundred & fifty dolles to Prospect to send Nellie[2] to School
Col Mudgett brought me out some clothes from Wheelwright & Clark[3]
($77,00) which I now owe them for. I may owe besides this perhaps
twenty five dollars. At the end of this month I shall have over four hundred & fifty dollars, & shall try & send you a check for four hundred,
which will leave three hundred after paying my bills. I believe I owe you
something near a hundred. Do I not? This then will leave two hundred I
shall be able now to send you in the future either a hundred a month or
two hundred & fifty every two months. I desire to be able to save enough
to keep me for a year after leaving the service—if not more—& by that
time I hope to be able to be established in a practise that will support me.
We are all hoping to hear of the Army being in Richmond. The Convention meets day after tomorrow & we all here predict a renomination,
which will be decided before you get this. I do not recollect whether I
wrote you or not that I sent you & Charlie each a karat of tobacco. It is
Parique the best kind known cut it across the end. Let me know how you
like it. It is only made in this part of the country. It is worth in New Orleans ten dollars a karat.

Your obst son
Cyrus Hamlin

On July 25, Cyrus's friend Colonel Appleton, after trying without
success to get transferred to General Butler's command in the East, re-
signed from the service. His regiment, now called the Eighty-first United
States Colored Infantry, had been consolidated with several other black
regiments, which, as Appleton noted in his letter of resignation, "renders
my presence here supernumerary." There seemed to be no point in stay-
ing on.[4]

The consolidation order almost induced Cyrus to quit as well, but
the day after Appleton resigned, Cyrus learned that his and Appleton's
regiments would be exempted from the order. Cyrus elected to stay put.
Remaining meant the possibility of facing one of the boards of examina-
tion that the War Department had established to ensure that the black
regiments had competent officers.

Heiad Quarters Bonnet Carre District
Bonnet Carre July 26. 1864

My Dear Father.

I received your letter of the 10th several days since but have delayed
writing you on account of an Order which I enclose. the issue of which,
has caused great consternation in our Corps. Many of the best Officers
sent in their resignation but none were accepted. The Board for the examination of us was organized yesterday with Genl Nickerson as Prest.
We have been in a State of Suspense whether to try & pass or all be re-
jected & go home, for our Status has been changed so many times we are
getting Sick & disgusted. I had almost made up my mind to return home
& for this purpose see Genl Banks & get him to accept my resignation as
a personal favor. but today I received a letter from one of my Lt[s] at New
Orleans who says the order will be Countermanded so far as not to effect
the Regts which have more than five hundred this will take Appletons &
my Regt (I have 640) with one other out of this order. I think I should
have been able to pass the board but I would not like to remain if the present Officers were not with me. but it is settled now & I shall not be at
home next month as I have been thinking. I was very much surprised to
hear of Prescotts death. he was one of my most intmate friends & I loved
him very much. I feel very sad & can hardly make myself realize that it is
so. My Command has been changed into a District & extends up the river
to Donaldsonville fifty miles from here. I am under Brig Genl T. W.
Sherman. I have only one Regt besides my own 11th N.Y. Cavalry known
as Scotts 900. I hear Genl Banks has asked to be relieved & that Genl
Reynolds is to be sent here. I like Genl R— very much. I wrote you some
time since about my money affairs & as the mails—two—were lost have
not heard from you about it—nor about the Pony at the Bangor House.

We have not been paid off. I shall have three months due me in a few days, if I can get it all I shall send five hundred to you. After paying what I owe I want you to invest it for me in Real estate or what ever you may think best. I see by the papers that you have been promoted to Corporal of the Color Guard.[5] What kind of Tactics do you use? Casey says "In battalions with less than five companies present, there will be no Color guard," A dispatch passed over the wires last night from Morganzia saying they expect a fight there to day. A Western Genl is in Com^d there— his name is Lawley, I think—Genl Ullmann is also there with five Regts of Colord troops. reenforcements have been sent up today. Genl Sickles left for the North a few days since. I have a Gunboat anchor here every Saturday night it patrols from here to Donaldsonville It is Commanded by Lt [Comr] Wells he used to [*illegible*] & married a Portland lady, now lives in Iowa. he told me he carried to Bangor some of the materials to build the first Toll bridge up in the Parish of Ascension where I have some of my Cavalry Stationed I met two Maine men working a place— Baxter—says he knows you saw you in Portland last fall—& Towle from Somerset Co. One of my Officers told me that just a bove where they are stationed (18 miles from here) that there was a Smith from Bangor & was formely a lumber man. Most all of the Northern men who have been working places here are going to make a fortune if Cotton remains at the present prices although there is none that will get on an average more than a quarter of a bale to the acre. I had some idea of returning here for that purpose if I had left the service. I am engaged to Nellie Sanborn which I trust will meet your approbation I shall write Sarah tomorrow, as I have not written home since the issue of that order.

Your Affectionate son
Cyrus Hamlin

Things continued to look up for Cyrus. In addition to his transfer to Bonnet Carré, the independence of his regiment, and his engagement to Nellie, he heard unofficially that he had been promoted to brigadier general. In fact, President Lincoln requested his appointment, "if it consistently can be" made, on June 29.[6]

Bonnet Carre Aug 4 1864.

My Dear Father.

I wrote Mother this afternoon but on reading your letter again this Eve, the thought came to me that as the Prest had ordered my promotion to be made, that perhaps the Commission or Appointment has been made & sent but may have been in the mail of one of the two Steamers which

sailed from New York about that time—one of them sunk at sea & the
other was captured by the Flordia—for New Orleans. Can not you find
out in some way if my conjecture may be true or not? I am very sorry to
hear of your loss & am glad that it was not more.[7] It is going on five
months since we were paid so I have not yet sent you any money. My
Regt with one exception is the largest in the Dept. over nine hundred.

Your affection Son
Cyrus Hamlin

*Cyrus's official reports from Bonnet Carré show little military activ-
ity: a few skirmishes, an occasional report of guerillas in the area. The
only real excitement occurred at Doyal's Plantation on August 5, when a
rebel force at first thought to number six hundred and later estimated at
1,500 surprised a portion of the 11th New York Cavalry and took ninety
or so prisoners and 130 horses.[8]*

*Cyrus's relations with his superiors remained tense. In May 1864,
Major General Edward R. S. Canby assumed command of the new Military Division of West Mississippi, which included the Departments of
Arkansas and the Gulf. In September, Banks went to Washington on a
twenty-day leave, but he stayed for months and in October was succeeded in command of the Department of the Gulf by Major General
Stephen Hurlbut. On October 7, Hurlbut revoked Cyrus's authority to
recruit blacks from the local plantations, ordering that no recruiting be
done "except on special permission, and then the recruits will be sent to
the General Rendezvous for equitable distribution."[9]*

*On October 18, Hurlbut's Special Order No. 282 placed General
Andrews in command of the United States Colored Troops in the Department of the Gulf. The three divisions were to be headed by Ullmann
(two brigades), Colonel Charles W. Drew (two brigades), and Cyrus
(three brigades).[10] On November 10, Cyrus issued an order announcing
his assumption of command. In the following letter, Cyrus describes activities related to the new position and also hints at some bitterness toward William Pitt Fessenden. The Maine legislature was due to choose a
United States senator in January 1865. Hannibal Hamlin, having been
replaced on the Republican national ticket by Andrew Johnson, seemed
to have the election sewn up until Fessenden spoiled his plans. One of
Maine's leading Whigs before joining the Republican Party, Fessenden
had resigned from the Senate to become secretary of the treasury, but he
soon desired to return to the Senate and began to elbow Hamlin aside.
Cyrus's displeasure with Fessenden no doubt stemmed as much from the
secretary's political machinations as from his unwillingness to help
Cyrus get a promotion.*

Headquarters 3d Division U. S. Colored Troops,
Department of the Gulf,
New Orleans Nov 25th 1864

My Dear Father,

I think I wrote Sis that I had been placed in command of this Division, since then I have been to Port Hudson & Bonnet Carre, returned here ten days ago. I have as yet but little to do, but on the first of next month expect to have enough to keep us busy. I have Maj Mudgett & Lt Wing with me, as I want to divide my Staff among the Brigades I have as yet selected only these with me. We have been trying to get in to our Office but will not be able before the first of next week. I have also been hunting for a furnished house but we have not been able to find one, the quartermaster can not furnish quarters, so we concluded that it will be the cheapest to keep house as Maj Mudgett expects his wife here & we have a number of servants, our communitation [*sic*] combined will pay the expense while it will not if we board. I am now stoping at the City Hotel but hope to be able to secure a house in a few days. Genl Canby is much better & will be about in a few weeks. There is a strong rumor here that Genl Banks is Sec of War. His friends expect him back here & I am inclined to think he will be here in a few days It is said if he comes here Canby will make his Hd Qts at Memphis. There is a very bitter feeling between them & I have no doubt something will be done about it before Banks returns. Hon T. A. D. Fessenden is here I saw him to day. he is stopping with Cuttler[11] the Cotton Agent for the Govt. I guess he came to make some money. I believe if I was out of the service I could make a handsome fortune in a short time but my position will not allow me to do any thing. I wish you would send me a letter of introduction to Genl Canby. I would like to call on him some time. I hear various reports about the Senatorial question, the news we have from the North today are that Fessenden will be returned to the Senate. I wish you would tell me if you are sure of your election I looked over the members [*illegible*] elect to the Legislature, those I knew, were once your friends & I hope are now.[12] I wrote Pickard some two months ago to ask Fessenden to speak to the President about my promotion but he said that as long as Morrill had the matter in hand he (Fessenden) better not do any thing. Well, perhaps there may yet be a day when he may wish aid. I shall write Morrill when I get settled & inclose a copy of the order assigning me to duty to place with the other papers. I have often thought that I would have demanded of the President if I had been in your position, that at least some of the patronage should have been given & placed at your disposal. I have been told the Breckinridge had one fourth at his disposal—but you know much better than I what not only is best but right. Yesterday was Thanksgivin here, I would have liked to have been at home that day more than any other in the year. Where is Charlie It is a long time since I heard from him.

Love to all
Your affectionate son
Cyrus Hamlin
P.S.
Please direct to me
Lock Box 522.
N.O.
CH

For a few months, Cyrus's Third Division included the Ninety-seventh U.S. Colored Infantry. On December 4, 1864, Major Lewis P. Mudgett, as the division's inspection officer, reported that the Ninety-seventh was unkempt in appearance, had been "constantly employed on fortifications," and was "very deficient in drill and discipline." Mudgett attributed the regiment's poor shape to the "intention rather than the inefficiency of commanding officers."[13] Cyrus could hardly be blamed for the policy of his superiors to use black soldiers as laborers rather than fighters or for the attitude of the regiment's officers before the Ninety-seventh came under his command. But apparently, in six weeks, his Third Division had done little to improve the regiment's condition.

In December, Cyrus finally received his promotion to brigadier general. Despite the rumors he had heard the previous summer, his nomination did not go to the Senate until December 12 . Although the Senate did not formally approve the promotion until February, the nomination by the president was all Cyrus needed to start organizing his division staff and proposing his successor as colonel of the Eightieth U.S.C.T.[14]

Headquarters 3d Division U. S. Colored Troops,
Department of the Gulf,
New Orleans Dec 27th 1864

My Dear Father.

This is the first time I have had since I received your letter to write you. I have been visiting different points of the State inspecting my command. What time I have been in the City I have been quite busy in my office. I now have a nice furnished house, got into it yesterday. It is assigned to me for my quarters. Maj Mudgett & Lt Wing are with me, they draw commutation for fuel & quarters & turn it in for the mess, this we are in hopes will pay our expenses

The first news I had of my promotion cam by Charlis letter. I got my appointment the same day at Gen Canbys Hd. Qts. I was very much surprised as well as pleased, for it. My promotion makes a vacancy in the Regt & I am very anxious that Lt Col William S. Mudgett should succeed me as the Col of the 80 U.S.C. Inf. It is due to him that he should have it, for he has been in command of since its organization you know he came out with me & has always been with the Regt & is entitled to great credit for his service & kindness to me—& here I wish to say, that there has never been any thing but the best of feelings with all the officers in the Regt toward me, every thing has been harmonious & plesant I shall always look back upon this with pleasure, having seen so much internal troubles in other Regts—The Officers are all very anxious to have Mudgett promoted & he deserves it. I think if you will see the Sec of War & state to him what you know of Col Mudgett also, he is the Senior Lt Col here, he will Commission him or give him the Appointment as Col. they may refer the matter to Genl Thomas if so please write him & request him to give it to Col Mudgett.

I shall write Mother & Charlie as soon as I return from Ft Jackson where I am going tomorrow Mr Morse (keeps the City Hotel) returned from Maine yesterday & says your relection is certain, he told T. A. D. Fessenden so. I hope & pray it is so. The weather is warmer, like our Spring.

Your obt Son
Cyrus Hamlin

Cyrus's promotion meant a return to Port Hudson, where General Hamlin assumed command on February 20.

Head Quarters, U. S. Forces,
Port Hudson, La., Feb 21 1865

My Dear Father.

I arrived here on Sunday Eve & on Monday assumed Command, relieving Brig Genl Pile. Genl Andrews is to take the field with Genl Canby & this broke up our Corps. There is one Division of Colrd Troops going under Brig Genl Hawkins but they are Regts raised up the river. I judge this to be a very important movement, as a great many troops have come down the river, & are concentrated at Barrancas I hear Genl A. J. Smith who passed here last night is to have command, & perhaps Canby is to take the field himself. Everything is very quiet here, no force of any amount in this vicinity. I am very busy in looking over matters here, hope to get settled in a few days.

> In haste
> Your affection son
> *Cyrus Hamlin*

Cyrus's forces at Port Hudson consisted at first of the Seventy-eighth and Eighty-first U.S.C.T., the Fourth U.S. Colored Cavalry, and two batteries of light artillery. The outfits under his command would change constantly. Between February 28 and April 30, for example, he lost the Seventy-eighth U.S.C.T. but picked up the Fifty-fifth U.S.C.T. and a company of heavy artillery. Troop strength was perhaps 1,200 in March but grew as the war wound down and other military districts were discontinued.

Things stayed quiet at Port Hudson for the remainder of the war, disturbed only by occasional minor skirmishing and an expedition to Jackson.[15]

> HEADQUARTERS DISTRICT OF PORT HUDSON
> *Port Hudson, La., April 19, 1865*

Capt. WILLIAM H. CLAPP
Assistant Adjutant-General, Northern Division of Louisiana:

CAPTAIN: I have the honor to report that on the evening of the 17th, at 12 midnight, I left this post for Jackson with the Fourth Regiment U. S. Colored Cavalry and one section of the Twelfth Massachusetts Battery. I entered Jackson at daybreak; captured Captain Lipscomb, commanding the place, and one Confederate soldier. I met with no force of any description. Received intelligence that Colonel Griffith with his command was stationed six miles this side of Liberty. I am of the opinion that the remaining force of Confederates in that vicinity are ordered away, as Captain Lipscomb had orders to report at Macon and I found documents ordering what he considered his most reliable scouts and couriers to report to Colonel Gober at Clinton. I returned on the morning of the 18th without having a shot fired. I send Captain Lipscomb to you. Will send you the other prisoners at my earliest convenience.

I have the honor to be, very respectfully, your obedient servant,

> CYRUS HAMLIN,
> *Brigadier-General of Volunteers, Commanding*

Then came the terrible news of Lincoln's assassination. General Hamlin informed his men of the murder on April 20, 1865, predicting that "future history will call [Lincoln] the most loved and revered man of our nation."[16] Cyrus's letter to his father of April 23, 1865, telling the man who until recently had been next in line to the presidency how he had received the news, characteristically mingles the profound and the mundane, the public and the personal, seeming not to distinguish between strawberries and death.

HEAD-QUARTERS, UNITED STATES FORCES,
Port Hudson, La., April 23[d] 1865.

My Dear Father.

We were all rejoicing at the glorious news from the success of our Armies, & looking forward to the close of our struggle, when the sad news of the assassination of Sec Seward[17] & the murder of the President reached us. I can not express the feelings which took possession of us here, I do not think a reverse of our arms could have given us such a shock. every one seems to feel as if it is a personal as well as public loss, & I trust that good may come of it rather than evil.

Genl Banks assumed command yesterday[18] & I suppose as far as he can will persue a liberal policy towards trade I was supprised at the number of friends he has here, perhaps more than he has in the North.

I made a raid a week ago tonight to Jackson La. I succeeding in capturing two Capts & one Lieut which will break up the small squads which have been scouting around me I hope to finish a new work which I am building in a month then the garrison will be reduced if not before.

How long I shall continue in the service I can not say for I am liable to be mustered out at any day as I do not see the necessity of keeping me any longer. It may be that I may be kept for some time, having risen from the Colrd Troops & the probability is that they will be kept in the service. In case I leave the service I shall have a thousand dollars—the Govt owes me more than that now—which I think will support me until I have established myself in business. I saw that Genl Butler is to resume his [law] practise again. I had half a mind to write him & ask him if he wanted a partner on his own terms, but concluded to write you first

Did you ever know Miles Taylor, he has been in Congress from here. I do not know him personaly, but I have learned that he has been a conservative man, has had his sympathies with the South, but is a very honorable man. he is practising law law [sic] in New Orleans. I have thought of seeing him & see if I could not enter the practise here with him. I believe this is going to be a good opening for a young man, but it may take a long time before an extensive practise can be acquired, There are a great many claims[19] here which will pay well, when, if ever any thing is obtained. What can I do North, where is there an opening that I could do

any thing? If I had money I would purchase me a farm & with my practise I could but succeed most any where. My inclination & taste makes
me prefer the North & where I could be near you I had rather enter into
business with Charlie than anyone in the world, but the fees are larger
here & a fortune might be amassed here quicker. I have sometimes
thought that Charlie & I might start at Bangor provided you would enter
the pracitise again & with us, which would give sufficient business, & as
much as we could wish. I wish you would write me fully what you think
I had better do. I have never taken any important step in life without asking your advice, & I trust you will never think me to old to give it me, at
all times, & I do not know as I shall get over the habit of asking it of you.
I shall be twenty eight years old on the 26 inst,[20] I shall probably remaine
here for a month longer anyway whether I am in the service or out. I have
one valuable horse, which I shall bring North when I come. I have had
him since I have been here & I love him to well to part with him.

Love to all
Your affectionate son
Cyrus Hamlin

P.S. I meant to tell you I have had strawberries twice & [*illegible*]
once. Maj. L. P. Mudgett was killed on the 9th inst while leading his Regt
in a charge on Ft Blakely at Mobile, he was shot through the head and
died instantly

April 24. [1865]

Dear Father.

After finishing my letter I wrote the enclosed. I wish you to hand it
to either Wheeler or Lynde[21] If they see fit to publish it will you please
send a copy of it to Mrs L. P. Mudgett care of Hon. N. G. Hichborn
Stockton

Your Affectionate son
Cyrus Hamlin

P.S.

There is a rumor that Kirby Smith has sent down Commissioners today for the purpose of surrendering. I believe it

C.H.

*The horse that Cyrus loved so well was probably Jess, a white Mor-
gan mare he had captured in western Virginia and brought to Maine
after the war. When he decided to settle in New Orleans, he asked his
father to take care of Jess, which the elder Hamlin did for many years.*[22]
With the war about over, Cyrus's thoughts turned more and more to his

own future. Many young Union officers stationed in Louisiana chose to stay after the war and become businessmen, planters, or office-holders. Some, as Cyrus suggests in the following letter to Charlie, got a head start, speculating in cotton or other commodities while still in uniform. Cyrus alludes in the letter to some matter that angered him, but provides no clue as to its nature. Perhaps it was a revelation about the previous fall's Republican convention that had replaced his father with Andrew Johnson on the national ticket. In any event, at this early date in Johnson's presidency, Cyrus bore no ill will toward the new chief executive. His hopes for Johnson would soon be dashed.

Head-Quarters, United States Forces,
Port Hudson, La., April 26 1865.

My Dear Brother.

I have just received yours of the 12 inst.

It is the first thing I have heard of anything about the matters refered to by you. I did not know before the true cause but it makes me mad. & I will yet live to see the day to pay such men for their ingratitude & baseness.

How long I shall continue in the service you can judge as well as myself. but I shall remaine now until such time as I may be ordered to be mustered out. for I shall need what money shall get, for future use. which will support me until I have sufficient business or obtain some thing which will give me a livelyhood

I think I might have made money like many others, but I have not & do not regret that I did not do it. Most probably I shall be at home before many months & then I shall decide what to do, if not before.

Every thing is very quiet here If a movement is made on Texas I do not expect to be in it, as this place will be held for some time to come & they will keep me here.

The Rebel ram Webb passed here Sunday in the night, having escaped from Red River the telegraph wires were cut & she went to New Orleans without meeting any resistance, she had our flag flying until she got most by that city when she hoisted the Reb flag. a gunboat followed her & when about twenty miles below, she was injured so that they ran her a shore & set her on fire she had over two hundred bales of cotton & probably was endeavouring to get to Matamoras.

What do you think of Johnson has it [*sic*] not got more backbone than Lincoln had & will not he be inclined to deal to Davis & Co the full extent of the law? I trust so for after all the struggles which we have passed through, I think a little hemp will but meet the demands of the army. [23]

I suppose Father & Johnson are on good terms, for they were in [*il-legible*].[24]

I will write you often & I wish you to do the same.

Love to all
Your affectionate brother
Cyrus Hamlin

P.S.

I forgot to tell you that today is my Birthday I am twenty eight years old.[25] I wrote Father last Sunday about settling here What do you think about it.

C.H.

There is a gap of several months in Cyrus's surviving correspondence. During that time he seems to have remained in command at a quiet Port Hudson until August, while contemplating the possibility of working under General O. O. Howard of Maine during the reconstruction of the Union. Howard had been appointed commissioner of the Freedmen's Bureau, a federal agency created by Congress on March 3, 1865, and designed to help the former slaves adjust to freedom. Howard had authority to appoint ten assistant commissioners.

Head-Quarters, United States Forces.
Port Hudson, La. Aug 15, 1865.

My Dear Father.

I have just received an order, ordering me to proceed to my residence & report to the Adjt. Genl.

I leave here Sunday & intend to sail from New Orleans Wednesday the 23. & shall be in New York on or about the 1st of Sept. I will telegraph you when I will be in Bangor. As I have not heard from you I shall take my horse with me, (one I leave here as I intend to return & work a plantation next season My hope is to get detailed under Genl Howard

Your obet son
Cyrus Hamlin

Brother Charles thought Cyrus would make an admirable administrator under Howard, as he wrote Hannibal Hamlin from Washington in a letter of August 28, 1865.

Received a letter from Cy. who has got his order to go to his home & report to the Adjutant General of the Army by letter. This is preparatory to be mustered out. He speaks of his desire to remain in the service (until spring) by getting a place in General Howards Bureau—that he will telegraph for permission—as soon as he arrives—to come here to see Howard.

I have hopes that Howard will do something for him *if he knew you* desire it. Two openings present themselves—Commissioner of Louisiana or Asst. Comm. of Texas under General Gregory. Cy. says the colored people in New Orleans have petitioned Howard to appoint him for La. (unbeknown to him) but I am inclined to think the General if inclined to do anything for him would prefer to give him the Asst. Comr under Gregory in Texas.

Howard is expected to return here from Chicago on Thursday of this week when I shall see him

Consider the propriety of telegraphing Howard for Cy and I will attend to it. Cy. will return South to engage in running a plantation and in the meantime it is a question about which I have no doubt Genl Howard could find no more efficient available enthusiastic or desirable Assistant than Cyrus—He represents Conway the Com. for La. as not *the* man for the place.

According to Charlie's letter, Cyrus left New Orleans for New York on August 23. If Howard offered Cyrus a position, Cyrus did not take it. He appears to have spent the next few months in Bangor looking after the affairs of his father, who had been appointed collector of the Port of Boston.

Bangor Dec 6th 1865

My Dear Father.

Mr Kilgore called to see me & says he has found a purchaser for the property at Hampden He has been at H— & seen the house & is much pleased with it. His name is Wm S. Harriman a returned Californian. Mr K. told him you asked $2500.00. he wished Mr. K. to write to you & get you to write him your lowest figure—the trade will be cash down. So you had better write Mr Harriman (& direct your letter to this place) immediately to close it up. Mr. K. wishes you to write him the same time what you write Harriman he is a young man & has no family. Will not want posession until spring if you desire to occupy until that time. Mr K thinks you had better close it at once

I rode down home yesterday, all well. Sis & Nellie came up & went to an Assemblie with me last Eve. They went back this morn.

The weather is growing cold, have about two inches of snow

The river will close up in a few days, it is now full of ice.

Your obj son
Cyrus Hamlin

Bangor Dec 20. 1865

My Dear Father

I received your letter Saturday Eve & immediately wrote Mr Brown that I would attend to any business for him. I do not know when I shall go South, as it depends upon my being mustered out, I shall leave immediatly after that. Mr Fitz[26] writes me that owing to the very heavy wind after I left, he lost one third of his crop, yet he has made a clear profit of ten thousand dollars. he is anxious for my return, & says there are fine opportunities to make money.

I have been thinking if they increase the Regular Army I might obtaine a field position & for that purpose I might secure letters of a general character from Genl Officers, & Members of Congress & put them on file What do you think of it?

I was very much pleased to receive the appointment of Bvt. Maj. Genl. Vols. on the 15 inst to date the 13 of March. This is, I believe to be the work of the Sec, which I believe, to be wholy unsolicted by any one, for me. I wish you would please ask George to send me a pair of Maj. Genls Straps. I do not want any thing expensive, but a neat, plain, small strap. Send them by Express.

Love to all
Your affectionate Son
Cyrus Hamlin

NOTES

1. *OR*, ser. 1, vol. 34, pt. 3, p. 194.

2. "Nellie" may have been Mary Ellen Sanborn, the younger sister of Cyrus's deceased wife, Sarah L. Sanborn. Mary Ellen appears in the 1850 census as the four-year-old daughter of Sarah Sanborn of Prospect, Maine. No father is listed. In the 1860 census, Sarah appears in the household of Weston B. Nutter of Prospect, along with Sarah L. and Mary Ellen.

3. Wheelwright, Clark, & Co. was a dry-goods dealer in Bangor, Maine.

4. David M. Gold, "Frustrated Glory: John Francis Appleton and Black Soldiers in the Civil War," *Maine Historical Society Quarterly*, 31 (Summer 1991): 198.

5. With no influence on the Lincoln administration and nothing to do in Washington, Hannibal Hamlin spent the summer of 1864 in Maine. He had enlisted as a private in the state coast guard in 1861. Called to active duty and promoted to corporal, he served for two months with his unit in Kittery.

6. Roy P. Basler, ed., *The Collected Works of Abraham Lincoln* (New Brunswick, N.J.: Rutgers University Press, 1953), 7:416.

7. Hannibal Hamlin estimated the loss from a fire in his stable in Bangor to be five or six hundred dollars. H. Draper Hunt, *Hamlin: Lincoln's First Vice President* (Syracuse: Syracuse University Press, 1969), 168.

8. *OR*, ser. 1, vol. 41, pt. 1, pp. 214-18.

9. Records of the Adjutant General's Office, 1780's-1917, General's Papers, Daniel Ullmann, Record Group 94, National Archives and Records Administration, Washington, D.C. The order establishing the Bureau of Colored Troops in 1863 prohibited the recruitment of colored troops except as specially authorized by the War Department. *OR*, ser. 3, vol. 3, p. 215.

10. *OR*, ser. 1, vol. 41, pt. 4, p. 68.

11. In 1864, Congress authorized the secretary of the treasury to appoint purchasing agents for the federal government in the rebellious states. Otis N. Cutler was the purchasing agent in New Orleans. *Cutler v. Kouns*, 110 U.S. 720 (1884).

12. Having been replaced on the Republican national ticket by Andrew Johnson, Hannibal Hamlin hoped to be elected to the United States Senate by the Maine legislature. (Until 1913, state legislatures elected U.S. senators.) However, the legislators chose Secretary of the Treasury and former senator William Pitt Fessenden. In 1869, they elected Hamlin over Lot M. Morrill to fill Maine's other Senate seat.

13. Keith P. Wilson, *Campfires of Freedom: The Camp Life of Black Soldiers During the Civil War* (Kent, Ohio: Kent State University Press, 2002), 43.

14. *Senate Executive Journal*, 38th Cong., 2d sess., January 6, 1865, 41; ibid., February 14, 1865, 161.

15. *OR*, ser. 1, vol. 48, pt. 2, p. 124.

16. *OR*, ser. 1, vol. 48, pt. 2, pp. 136-37

17. Secretary of State William H. Seward was severely wounded as part of the same plot that resulted in Abraham Lincoln's death.

18. Banks returned from his extended leave on April 22, 1865, exercising limited authority over civilian government in New Orleans until May 17, when a reorganization of the military departments of the South by President Johnson deprived him of all authority. James G. Hollandsworth, Jr., *Pretense of Glory: The Life of General Nathaniel P. Banks* (Baton Rouge: Louisiana State University Press, 1998), 219-20.

19. The business of presenting claims against the government boomed during and after the Civil War, to the extent that in 1866 law-book author George W. Raff published *The War Claimant's Guide: A Manual of Laws, Regulations, Instructions, Forms and Official Decisions* (Cincinnati: R. Clarke, 1866), devoted exclusively to the prosecution of claims relating to pensions, bounties, lost and destroyed property, and other matters growing out of the conflict.

20. By all accounts, Cyrus was born in 1839, which would have made him twenty-six on April 26, 1865. He again stated that he was twenty-eight in his letter to Charlie of April 26, 1865.

21. Wheeler and Lynde published the *Bangor Daily Whig and Courier.* Hamlin's letter announcing Mudgett's death appeared anonymously in the paper on May 11, 1865.

22. Charles Eugene Hamlin, *The Life and Times of Hannibal Hamlin* (1899; repr., Port Washington, N.Y.: Kennikat Press, 1971), 2:575-76.

23. During the 1864 presidential campaign and after Lincoln's assassination, Johnson spoke forcefully of hanging rebels and traitors, but his Reconstruction policies disappointed Radical Republicans.

24. Cyrus used an illegible abbreviation at this point, but by a stretch of the imagination, it could be understood as meaning "Congress." Hannibal Hamlin and Andrew Johnson served together in the U.S. House of Representatives in the 1840s and in the U.S. Senate in the 1850s. In 1858, Hamlin and Johnson boarded at the same hotel. Hans L. Trefousse, *Andrew Johnson: A Biography* (New York: Norton, 1989), 56, 115.

25. See note 20, above.

26. Cyrus had a partner named Henry E. Fitz in a saddle business. Alanson B. Long to Hannibal Hamlin, November 12, 1867, HFP. A Civil War veteran of that name who later worked as a clerk in the United States Senate was one of Hannibal Hamlin's "oldest friends." *New York Times,* April 24, 1879; Hannibal Hamlin to Henry E. Fitz, February 23, 1881, February 28, 1881, HFP; Hunt, *Hamlin,* 216, 273n78.

Chapter Seven

Reconstruction Politics in New Orleans

Cyrus was mustered out of the service on January 15, 1866. By the middle of that year, he had returned to New Orleans and formed a partnership with Henry E. Fitz, a fellow New Englander, in the saddle business. Cyrus also made connections with some of the leading lawyers in the city. Federal District Court judge Edward H. Durell took Cyrus under his wing. Born in New Hampshire in 1810, Durell had moved to New Orleans in 1837, remained loyal to the Union, and been appointed judge in 1863, after Federal forces occupied the city. Durell's friend Edward C. Billings, who would succeed Durell as judge in 1876, also took an interest in Cyrus. Another Yankee lawyer, Billings belonged to the firm of Sullivan, Billings & Hughes. He came to New Orleans in 1865 at the age of thirty-six, supposedly for reasons of health. Young Cyrus had little to offer such high-profile figures in the way of legal experience or intellectual accomplishments, but Hannibal Hamlin appears to have known Billings and Cyrus apparently met Durell in New York City during the war.

Cyrus may also have had a flair for politics, and he certainly enjoyed links to power. (Former vice president Hannibal Hamlin was then working successfully toward reelection to the U.S. Senate.) While trying to get established in the practice of law, Cyrus cultivated his connections in New Orleans and followed political events closely. The constitutional convention of 1864, presided over by Durell, had adjourned with Unionists in control of the state government and hopes that blacks would soon receive political rights. When Andrew Johnson succeeded the murdered Lincoln as president, he let it be know that he would not press for political reform and civil rights. Former secessionists and their sympathizers, more rabid than ever in their hatred of blacks and Yankees, soon reasserted their control over the state legislature and city government. James M. Wells, a Louisiana planter who served as lieutenant governor under Michael Hahn, became chief executive in March 1865 when Hahn resigned to pursue a seat in the U.S. Senate. A Unionist who had little sympathy for black suffrage, Wells quickly turned his back on his erstwhile moderate and radical allies and made overtures to the Confederate veterans in the electorate. However, the lawmakers had no use for the Un-

ionist governor and enacted legislation intended to keep African Ameri-
cans subservient and to sweep Unionists out of government.

    Alarmed by the turn of events, leading Unionists and friends of
blacks sought to reconvene the constitutional convention in order to se-
cure black suffrage. The convention had adjourned subject to the author-
ity of the convention president to reconvoke the body, but less than a
quorum of delegates appeared at a preliminary meeting on June 26, and
Durrell, the president, refused to take part. Wells then supported another
attempt to reconvene on July 30 at the Mechanics' Institute on Dryades
Street. That meeting was just five days away when Cyrus wrote the fol-
lowing letter.

New Orleans July 25 1866.

My Dear Father.

    I have delayed writing you until I could hear from Washington from
Judge Durell Mr. Billings & Sullivan, they desired me to apply for the
position of U. S. Dist Atty, here, Mr. Goodloe the present Atty (of Ky), is
sick with the consumption & will probably never returne, I gave to Judge
Durell—born in N. H.—a letter of introduction to you & requested him
to call upon you as he passes through Boston. He has been a thorough
union man, has resided here for twenty eight years, & always denounced
the institution of Slavery. As far as I have been able to learn B. F. Flanders, Thomas J. Durant & Judge Durell are the only men in this State that
have *always been true* to the Govt & the Union. Judge Durell was Prest
of the Constitutional Convention of this State in 1864. You will recollect
that one great object of this Convention was to create an impression
abroad, that we were steadily suppressing the rebellion & the States were
being brought back to their former Status. When the Convention adjourned it adjourned subject to the call of its Prest—Hann was elected
Gov, then Senator which made J. M. Wells Gov. who sold out the Union
party which put him in power, by turning out all the Union men in office
& putting in Rebels who now have complete control of the State & have
thrown Wells overboard. They have an organization which no one is allowed to join unless he remained in the Rebel service up to the time of its
surrender or who was honorably discharged, they will not support any
one & ignore all others, unless he possesses these qualifications. Gov
Wells was very anxious to have Judge Durell reconvene the Convention
also Pierré Soulé & such men as done all they could to get the State to
secede but kept out of their armies so are ignored by the now
cont[r]olling powers then there are many good Union men who join with
them, but are in reality lead by them as well as for the spoils of Office.
Judge Durell at first agreed to reassemble the Convention if Gov Well

would write him a letter asking him to do so which he did. Judge D—
then applied to Genl Sherridan for military protection but he was not able
to grant it. While deliberating upon this the ReConstruction Comtte[1]
made their report, which wholy ignores the Present State Govt. it being
or having sprung from military power. on account of this Judge Durell
refused to reassemble the Convention, as he thought it would do no good.
but he was willing to go to Washington or they might send some one & if
there was any hope that they would be sustained he would assemble the
Convention, this they would not accept & he has been denounced as not
being true to the Union Cause. Billings & I have both stood by him &
endorse his course. Less than a quorum of the members met & requested
him as Prest of the Convention to meet them, he refused to do it, they
then declared his office vacant & elected R. K. Howell—Associate Judge
of the Supreme Court—Prest, pro tem, who has issued a call to the Convention to assemble on the 30 inst This is a statement of the facts as to
how the Convention is to be called. I think they have no right to call this
Convention together in this way for there is a doubt in some minds
wether or not Judge Durell could have done it legally. yet I think he
could have done so. Judge Durell has been very kind to me & takes an
interest in me. When the question came up who should take Goo[d]loes
place I was put forward & he said he would do everything in his power
for me. he, Sullivan & Billings are now in Washington. This morn, Judge
Hughes received a letter from Mr Ruse of [*illegible*], sending congratula-
tions to me as the future Dist Atty here. This is all done by Mr. Billings
who put my name forward for the position, he you will recollect meeting
several years ago in New York City. As a lawyer he has but one superior
here that is T. J. Durant Judge Durell says if nothing befalls him he will
stand at the head of our profession and next to Durant he leads the bar.
We have always been intimate since we boarded together in New York
City, the many kindness & services he has rendered me will never be
forgotten & if you can ever aid him or his friends, I shall feel very grate-
full for it. He will assist me in my duties whenever I need advice & Judge
Durell says I need have no fear as he will take care of me, this he said in
reply that I was not familliar to the practise & had been out of the law for
years. I am now in the office of Sullivan Billings & Hughes, a year & a
half ago they took in to their firm A. B. Long and gave him 1/7 interest,
his share has been over seven thousand dollars, they dissolved their
connection with him in June. Mr. Sullivan & Billings were obbliged to
go North, this left Judge Hughes alone here. Mr. B— on account of his
friendship to me proposed to them as Judge Hughes is liable to sudden
attacks of sickness, that during their absence I should come into their
office. So Mr. Sullivan proposed to me that during their absence I should
come into their office & assist Judge Hughes that they could not afford to

pay me much but on their return, if I did not obtain the U.S. Dist Atty-Ship, they would if I desired it give me the place in their firm that Long had. This I considered a very generous offer on their part & I at once accepted it & told Mr. Sullivan that so far as the compensation was concerned during their absence I did not care about that, as I would like to go into their office as I very much desired to read up, in order that I might again enter into my profession. I have been in their office a fortnight & shall remain here until they return, which will not probably be until Nov. In either case I think I have very flattering prospects for the future. I have very little to do in the office so I am able to devote most of my time to study. My Saddle business I have left in charge of a man who has always been in our employ. there is not much doing as it is very dull here but there will be a good market for them this Fall. S. Tyler Reed called on me yesterday said he called on you upon leaving Boston. he leaves for Mexico on Friday. I hope to be North during the Fall for the purpose of being married, but if my business does not permit I shall have to postpone it, although I hope I can take a vacation for three or four weeks after Mr. Billings & Sullivan returns.

Your Affectionate Son
Cyrus Hamlin

As Cyrus noted in his letter, the reconvening of the convention rested on a questionable legal foundation. Mayor John T. Monroe prepared to arrest the delegates on the ground that they threatened to subvert the government, and both supporters and opponents of the convention anticipated violence. On July 30, a parade of about two hundred black Union veterans encountered 1,500 or so white civilians and police outside the Mechanics' Institute, sparking one of the most vicious race riots in American history. Cyrus described it first in a letter to Daniel Ullmann[2] and then in correspondence with Hannibal Hamlin.

New Orleans Aug 17. 1866.

My Dear Genl.

Will you do me the favor to ask the Sec of War to appoint Capt Elbridge G. Manning 81 U.S.C. Infy to a Captaincy in one of the new Col[ore]d Regts which are to be raised. I think you will recollect him from having served so long on my Staff. He was at first my Commissary & since my Aid. I know of no officer better qualified, he served a short time as aid to Genl McNeil in Mo. where he was complimented in G. O. for gallant conduct on the field in leading a Cavalry charge. he has served over five years in the army, having enlisted in the 6 Mass Vol. Infty after in the 19th Regt before he was sixteen years of age, then joined us in New York.

If any are to be rewarded for faithful services, I truly know he is one

He could have been promoted at any time in his Regt. Col Appleton was anxious to make him a Capt. but he prefered to remaine with me as a Lieut & was promoted to Capt. on my being mustered out

While North last year I endeavoured to find you, but was unable to see you.

The 80 and 81 Regts are yet in the service I learn they are with the 82 to be mustered out on the first of next month These you will recollect comprised my old Brigade—with Jones Regt—when I served under you. I do not see as a more fitting compliment could be paid to us, than this, that they have been retained in the service until their term of service has expired. While other Regts whose time whould not have expired for months to come, were months ago mustered out.

We have passed through one of the most brutal & inhuman Riots that ever existed, history does not furnish a parallel. The Riot was a preconcerted plan to suppress the Convention, whether its assemblage was legal or not. The Police are or have been in the Rebel Army Mayor Monroe made not secrecy when appointing them that this qualification was required All trouble could have been prevented but this was not their object, they created the mob to suppress the Convention. The Sts could have been cleared without this murder & wholesale slaughter, if they had formed a line & swept the Sts, but instead they advanced & fired their revolvers & then retired. Colored men who came to the Police and asked protection were either shot by them or they allowed the thugs to do so & never did they interfere or try to prevent it, but encouraged it. I saw an old negro come runing down Canal St near Corondolet St. on the R. R track to get out of danger when a Policeman triped him up & shot him twice, while dying I saw a brute crush his head with a Stone, this I saw, I have heard of many other more brutal cases. I trust I may never pass through an other day like that. I trust the Commission which is investigating the matter may make public their finding.[3]

I am now in the Office of Sullivan Billings & Hughes, reading up in the law I may take a partnership with them in the Fall. If you or your friends have need of us at any time, be assured we will give our personal attention to any business which may be given us.

I am Genl
Your Obt. Servt.
Cyrus Hamlin

New Orleans Aug 19. 1866.

My Dear Father.

I commenced to write you a letter the day after the Riot here but I felt the effects of it so much that I did not finish it & what I wrote concluded to destroy.

I have seen death on the battle field but time will erase the effects of that, the wholesale slaughter & the little regard paid to human life I witnessed here on the 30 of July I shall never forget. I done all I could to persuade them not to call this Convention in manner it was done I tried to have it delayed but to no purpose. I did not agree with them although I wished the same result they were endeavoring to accomplish. Billings & I went to see Gov Wells—but he was out of Town—to persuade him to call the people togather & elect delegates to form a Constitution Convention & in his call to give the Col[ore]d man the right to vote, in this way we could secure the balance of power in it, but I do not know but it is quite as well, perhaps the result might have been the same as has happened to this one which did assemble.

I thought there would be trouble, so I did not go near the Institute but remained in the office, which is two & a half squares from Drayades St.[4] I could distinctly hear the firing & see the people run as they came on to Canal St. I saw men & boys passing with pistols & I saw the Police retire after discharging their revolvers I saw a Policeman trip a negro up in Canal St a bout a square from where I was & shoot him twice killing him instantly. I saw a brute then crush his head by throwing a stone on it. This is not more fiendish than other things which have been related to me by those who saw them.

This mob might have been prevented by having placed Policemen at the Corner of Sts & not allowed the people to have remained there, after it had commenced the Sts might have been cleared by fifty men by forming a line & marching up to the crowd which would dispersed it but this was not there object. they desired to suppress the Convention therefore they encouraged & aided to get up the Riot as they were unable to accomplish their desire except in this way.

Mayor Monroe made no secrecy that it was requiset that men should have served in the Rebel Army to obtain a place on the Police force.

The Police were many of them drunk & made their boasts how many they had killed, that they had got their revenge on the d— Yankee

Dr Dostie was killed by a Policeman after he was in the hands of the Police. Ex-Gov Hann & Shaw were wounded after the Police had taken charge of them, by the good law abiding citizens as the Press here endavours to explain it. The Press done all they could to creat it now, they strive to conceal the true facts. You have probably ere this seen a good description of it, perhaps better than I can give you.

Capt Elbridge G. Manning 81. U.S.C. Infty will be mustered out with his Regt. the first of next month. He desires an appointment as Capt in one of the new Col[ore]d Regts which are to be raised. I have written to Wilson & Sumner also to Genl Ullmann. Will you recommend him to the Sec of War for an appointment as Capt. I wrote Mr Stanton myself & think he will grant it if you but ask it. The weather is getting cooler, it has been exceedingly hot. I have not heard any thing from Washington but I believe if there is to be a change I shall succeed.

Your Affectionate Son
Cyrus Hamlin

The poisoned political and racial atmosphere of New Orleans portended ill fortune for Cyrus personally. His would-be law partners apparently decided that they could do without Cyrus's services. Perhaps he had little legal ability, or maybe he had become a political liability due his Radical Republican activities. His dignity affronted, Cyrus took the hint, but he held on to his political ambitions.

New Orleans Jan 17. 1867.

My Dear Brother

I have commenced to write you twice since I received your letter of the 23 inst, both times have been interrupted. I was very glad to hear from you & to learn that you are doing so well. I wish I could say the same of myself. on the first of the month I left Sullivan Billings & Hughes. they did not do by me as they had agreed when they returned from the North—S & B—they kept postponing the matter until H— return when he came, they thought that business was so dull that they could get along &c. I saw what they desired & told them that I had made up my mind that the best thing I could do was to start now for myself. I did not desire them to keep their agreement with me after this, knowing that it would be very uncomfortable for me if I held them to their agreement. So I have started for my self, hired an office & borrowd some law books & am not doing much of any thing as yet. I shall try it a year as I have money enough to live on for that time. I think by that time I shall be able to secure a paying practise. I have two cases in Court which will pay fifty dollars. I have one case to bring if I am successful will pay me one or two thousand dollars. I think there is no doubt but that I shall succeed. It is where a house at Port Hudson—now here—purchasing cotton of a Mr East agreed to give him New Orleans prices for his cotton & let him have goods at N. O. prices cost of transportation added, they claim that there was a settlement but my client says not. I do not care for the settlement for if there was one made it was in fraud. I shall show fraud in the price of goods where they charged more than three hundred per cent upon what was N. O. prices I shall also show that they returned false weights & thus they brought him in debt to them while they owe him some three to five thousand dollars. It is a hard matter to prove their contract but I think I shall be able to do it. They have admitted as to the price of the cotton but say that they never agreed as to the price of goods. I can show by one of their clerks that they all thought or at least the understanding that they— who were employed in the house—that it was as we say & that they made out a bill to my client upon the bill heads of another house in this city & added drayage & that this was done to convince my client that it was the bill rendered them for the house here & that it was New Orleans prices. I can also show they agreed to take cotton from other parti[e]s & return goods at N. O. prices. They can never render a bill again like the one given my client has as no entry was made on their books of it. I can also show that they mixed up their cotton so that it was impossible to give the correct weight to any one, that upon their reciving the list of weights they could not tell which belonged to my client but that they picked out so many bales & called it his I think I have got a good case. I have some two hundred bounty claims which I have forwarded through Chipman Hosmer Gilmore & Brown.[5] I could have had two or three thousand of them if I had made any exertion for them last Fall I have now had some blanks printed so that I procure them myself & get all the fee instead of half as I have been doing. I am bound to succeed here & have no fear but what I will do my share. I have sold out my saddle business for seven hundred & twenty five dollars. this is all I have left out of the thing except a living for the past year. I got three hundred down & a note for the balance. this is all I have. I would gladly let you have what you desire if I had it. You see what I have I send you a draft for one hundred upon receipt of which let me know as I have the duplicate I may be able to help you during the year which I will do if I can. So far as a note for it I dont want it. I want you all to feel that if I have any thing you want, that it is always yours. I know you have the same feeling towards me. I wish I had sufficient property that I might give it to Father so that he always be independent. He shall never suffer for any thing if I have any thing. What I have I would rather he had it. after all that he has done I dont like to see him feel as if he is oblidged to work. What is being done in relation to the Senatorship. Will he do any thing to secure it. I feel as if he could have it, if he would take hold & work as he use to. if he does not I fear that he will be cheated out of it. He is extremely popular with all men that I meet from all sections of the Country. It is too early to foretell who will be the Nominee for the President, the issues of today may so change that those men who are prominent today will have disappeared & some new man will come up. Yates of Ill is making a strong exertion & I judge is quite popular at the West. By the way did you ever get Adjt Genl Hodsdon report for me, if not I wish you would secure one for me & keep it until I come north. I shall not probably be north until the hot weather. I had intended to have been married this last Fall but have deferred it until my business will justify it. Give my love to Father Mother & all the dear ones at home. I wish you would write me oftener & keep me posted in Maine Matters. The rebs are jubilant over the Supreme Court decission.[6] I was in hopes they would give us a Military Govt. or its equivalent but I have almost given up in dispair. We are about forming a branch of the "Grand Army of the Republic"[7] which will give us an efficient organization. I shall go into it in order to be able to controll the delegation to the Conventions in the future. I have kept quiet heretofore but now I am going to take hold & have a hand in matters.

Your affectionate brother
Cyrus Hamlin

I had to pass an Examination here before I was admitted, we have no Common law it is Civil Law founded upon the Code Napoleon. all actions are brought in a petition very simple, setting forth the facts. it resembles common law in many respects but differs as to terms or names as for instance Contracts are "obligations" Probate matters are "Successions" &c. Some of it seems very repugnant to my ideas of justice.

C. H.

Despite the disappointing result of his association with Sullivan, Billings & Hughes, Cyrus decided to stick it out in New Orleans, busying himself with politics as well as law. As to the latter, he advertised his practice in the paper, listing his address as 13 St. Charles Street and naming as references six prominent Republicans: two United States senators, the governor and lieutenant governor of New York, a recent governor of Massachusetts, and a justice of the Maine Supreme Judicial Court.[8] Politically, Cyrus helped organize mass meetings at which he gave speeches and offered resolutions in support of the Radical Republican plan of Reconstruction and General Philip H. Sheridan's strict rule as military governor of Louisiana and Texas. In an address to a meeting of workingmen,[9] he attacked corruption in the municipal government of New Orleans, and he was elected to the council of administration of the Grand Army of the Republic's Department of Louisiana. Personal ambition no doubt played a role in all this activity, but so did principle. A friend described Cyrus as "a fearless advocate of the freedom of all" whose "long connection with the Corp D'Afrique had familiarized him with the sufferings of and the wrongs done the colored race."[10]

New Orleans May 29. 1867.

My Dear Father.

I received your letter of the 18 inst yesterday. enclosing one to you from Mr. Richardson.[11] I received a letter from him on the 24 inst, the first and only one, since I saw him in Boston. I ans it on the same day, giving him an account & remitting to him all the money due him to June I explaine to him why I had not done it before. which I think will be satisfactory when I went North I had not sufficient money in my hands, to pay expenses due from Storeage &c upon his things. The rent from Jan. I had not recd being in the hands of the Constable at Gretna, whome I employ to collect & look after his property although I was personally responsible for it to Mr Richardson. As I shall hereafter write him on the first of each month remitting whatever may be due. I hope to give you no cause of pain or trouble on account of my acts in the future. We are very busy in political matters. I am taking quite an active part in them. We are unfortunate in having a division among us. which arises more from those who want office than from any other cause At first the Colord men were greatly in the Majority on the registration lists. Their paper, upon that basis demanded that the party should pledge the party to support one half Colord men for positions. There were Southern union men who opposed this & thus a division came. As we must be united or we will loose every thing I have been trying, to harmonize every thing by endeavoring to put forth a principle & then agreeing to support all who may be regularly nominated, if they are honest & are educated sufficint to fill the position for which they may be nominated.[12] It will be some months before any election takes place except for a Convention, so that I believe all will comprehend that we must be a Unit to succeed. Some of my friends are desirous for me to be a candidate for Mayor, others desire that I shall go to the Convention & then to Congress for the (2ᵈ) Dist. in which I live. I have not yet made up my mind what I will run for. I think now that I stand a better change [*sic*] for Congress. As the matter stands to day it is difficult for me to decide. I shall not probably be North until our political matters are in a better status, it may be that I shall have to stay through the Summer. The most I desire is success & shall do all in my power to make it so. & if I am in the way at any time, shall decline taking any thing. I think I have a good prospect for the future, & I shall try to conduct myself so that I shall not loose it. Give my love to [all].

Your affectionate son
Cyrus Hamlin

Cyrus probably exaggerated his political influence; his name does not appear in studies of Louisiana politics during the immediate post-war years. On the other hand, being young, enthusiastic, and well-connected in Washington, his prospects may well have been sunny. He finally settled on attending the next state constitutional convention, scheduled to meet that year, and intended to prepare himself by reading the constitutions and constitutional convention proceedings of other states. After the convention, he might place his name before the people as a candidate for Congress.[13]

In July, reports of yellow fever in New Orleans began to appear in the papers. They grew progressively worse: two deaths on August 3, then twenty-three deaths within two days, then sixty-nine deaths in the week ending August 24.[14] Cyrus spent the evening of Saturday, August 24, working in his law office with his partner, C. C. Packard. At about three o'clock the next morning, he came down with a chill. By Monday, it was clear that he had yellow fever. Despite the anxious attentions of friends and the best medical care in the city, he could not be saved. On August 28, Packard telegraphed the news of Cyrus's death to Hannibal Hamlin. The next day, another friend wrote to Cyrus's father:[15]

Your loss Sir, is no doubt, great; we, his friends, have had taken from our midst, one, who by his courteous and gentlemanly conduct, has endeared himself to us; but the loss to this Country, is greater by far, than all our losses combined. I know of no one here, who will be able to replace him. His honesty, integrity and unselfish love of Country had gained for him the love and esteem of all who knew him.

Cyrus had an imposing funeral. A military band and members of Sheridan's staff attended the cortege. The mayor of New Orleans served as a pallbearer. Organizations to which Cyrus had belonged—the Masons, the Grand Army of the Republic, the Frederick Douglass Radical Republican Club—marched in the procession. During his illness, Cyrus had asked that his body be sent to Maine—"God's own country"—for burial in the family plot. Because fear of yellow fever and the hot, humid weather made immediate shipment impossible, James H. Ingraham, a mulatto, a captain in the Native Guards, and a leader in the fight for equality in Louisiana, offered the use of his tomb in the Girod Street cemetery. Packard took charge of Cyrus's estate and of arrangements to send the body back to Maine. On November 5, Cyrus began his last journey home.[16]

NOTES

1. Congress established the Joint Committee on Reconstruction in December 1865. The committee laid the foundations for a radical reconstruction of the South, in opposition to President Johnson's more lenient approach. On June 20, 1866, the committee issued its final report refusing to recognize any of the governments of the former Confederate states.

2. Cyrus Hamlin to Daniel Ullmann, August 17, 1866, Daniel Ullmann Papers, New-York Historical Society, New York.

3. The report of the military commission appointed to investigate the riot was published in the *New York Times* on October 4, 1866. The report concluded with a warning that the hostility of the party that controlled the city government toward Northern and Union men would soon pose a serious danger to their lives and property. However, the commission made no recommendations for action, leaving that matter to the political authorities.

4. Cyrus's office address was 178 Customhouse. L. Graham, comp., *Graham's Crescent City Directory for 1867* (New Orleans: L. Graham, 1867), 225. Customhouse ran parallel to Canal Street, one block to the east. Canal and Dryades intersected at the Mechanics' Institute.

5. Chipman, Hosmer, Gilmore & Brown was a prestigious Washington, D.C., law firm that handled many claims against the government. It was headed by Norton Parker Chipman (1834-1924), a colonel and chief of staff to Major General Samuel R. Curtis during the Civil War. As an army lawyer, Chipman prosecuted the commandant of the notorious Andersonville prison. He later represented Washington, D.C., in Congress and served as an appellate judge in California.

6. In *Ex Parte Milligan*, 71 U.S. 2 (1866), the U.S. Supreme Court held that civilians could not be tried in military courts in areas remote from the theater of war if civilian courts were open. The Court announced its decision in April, but the justices did not read their opinions until December 17. The opinions were published in full on January 1, 1867. Samuel Krauss, ed., *The Milligan Case* (New York: Knopf, 1929), 44, 47.

7. The Grand Army of the Republic was a national Union veterans' organization founded in 1866 to mobilize the soldier vote for the Republican Party and to further the interests of veterans. It quickly acquired great political influence.

8. *New Orleans Republican*, April 14, 1867, April 27, 1867, May 12, 1867.

9. Radical Republicans presented themselves as the champions of white workers as well as black freedmen and tried, unsuccessfully, to unite the two groups politically. Eric Arnesen, *Waterfront Workers of New Orleans: Race, Class and Politics, 1863-1923* (New York: Oxford University Press, 1991), 1-33.

10. *New Orleans Republican*, June 14, 1867, July 9, 1867; A. B. Long to Hannibal Hamlin, September 9, 1867, HFP.

11. After Cyrus's death, his law partner wrote to Hannibal Hamlin about claims against the business for merchandise sold by F. Richardson of Boston. C. C. Packard to Hannibal Hamlin, October 31, 1867, HFP.

12. With the support of the *Republican's* rival paper, the *Tribune*, the Republican party decided in June 1867 to allot one-half of all appointments and nominations to blacks. Jean-Charles Houzeau, *My Passage at the New Orleans Tribune: A Memoir of the Civil War Era*, ed. David C. Rankin, trans. Gerard F. Denault (Baton Rouge: Louisiana State University Press, 1984), 147-48.

13. John Charles O'Neill to Hannibal Hamlin, August 29, 1867, HFP.

14. *New Orleans Republican*, July 2, 1867, August 4, 1867, August 21, 1867, August 25, 1867.

15. Telegram, C. C. Packard to Hannibal Hamlin, August 28, 1867, HFP; O'Neill to Hannibal Hamlin, August 29, 1867, ibid.

16. *New Orleans Republican*, August 30, 1867; Edward H. Bean to Hannibal Hamlin, August 30, 1867, HFP.

Appendix

Information about many individuals in Cyrus Hamlin's cast of characters is readily accessible through standard reference works. In this appendix, I have identified most of the persons mentioned in the letters. Actual or approximate years of birth and death, when they could be ascertained, are included. In cases in which data from the standard reference works were meager or nonexistent, I resorted to a wide variety of sources, many of them found on the internet, to track down information. Sometimes, though, I drew a blank. A dedicated genealogist might have done better, but even a successful hunt for a few obscure individuals would have added little or nothing to the value of Hamlin's correspondence. The length of an identifying note and the number of sources cited have no necessary relationship to the historical importance of the person identified. Some prominent individuals whom Cyrus mentions in passing receive just a line. I have provided more information on two categories of persons: those who played a significant role in Cyrus's story and, where possible, those who are virtually unknown and about whom data are hard to find. Where one rank is given for a military figure, it is the person's rank as of the time he was mentioned in the correspondence. Unless otherwise indicated, every soldier was in the Union army.

Entries on individuals for whom I did not give a source may be found in one or more of these widely available reference works:

American National Biography, 24 vols. (New York: Oxford University Press, 1999)

Biographical Directory of the United States Congress, 1774-2005: The Continental Congress, September 5, 1774, to October 21, 1788, and the Congress of the United States, from the First through the One Hundred Eighth Congresses, March 4, 1789, to January 3, 2005, Inclusive (Washington, D.C.: GPO, 2005) (also accessible at bioguide.congress.gov)

Dictionary of American Biography, 20 vols. (New York: C. Scribner's Sons, 1928-1936)

Ezra Warner, *Generals in Blue: Lives of the Union Commanders* (Baton Rouge: Louisiana State University Press, 1964)

The following abbreviations are used for other sources:

BBGB	Roger D. Hunt and Jack R. Brown, *Brevet Brigadier Generals in Blue*, rev. ed. (Gaithersburg, Md.: Olde Soldier Books, 1997)
CWD	Historical Data Systems, American Civil War Research Database, http://www.civilwardata.com
DLB	Glenn R. Conrad, ed., *A Dictionary of Louisiana Biography*, 2 vols. (New Orleans: Louisiana Historical Association, 1988) (also available at http://www.lahistory.org/site.php)
HFP	Hamlin Family Papers, Special Collections, Raymond H. Fogler Library, University of Maine at Orono
L&T	Charles Eugene Hamlin, *The Life and Times of Hannibal Hamlin*, 2 vols. (1899; repr., Port Washington, N.Y.: Kennikat Press, 1971)
MR	Guy V. Henry, *Military Record of Civilian Appointments in the United States Army*, 2 vols. (New York: D. Van Nostrand, 1873), vol. 1
OAR	U.S. Adjutant General's Office, *Official Army Register of the Volunteer Force of the United States Army for the Years 1861, '62, '63, '64, '65*, 8 vols. (Washington, D.C.: U.S. War Department, 1865-1867), vol. 8
OR	U.S. War Department, *The War of the Rebellion: A Compilation of the Official Records of the Union and Confederate Armies*, 128 vols. (Washington, D.C.: GPO, 1880-1901) (also available at http://digital.library.cornell.edu/m/moawar)
"UB"	I. S. Bangs, "The Ullman [*sic*] Brigade," in *War Papers Read Before the Commandery of the State of Maine, Military Order of the Loyal Legion of the United States*, 2 (Portland, Maine: Lefavor-Tower, 1902): 289-310

Much of this book covers Cyrus Hamlin's experiences in organizing and leading black regiments. As observed in the preface, Daniel Ullmann's five regiments were the first African-American regiments to have the unequivocal approval of the War Department. Originally, they were referred to as the First through Fifth Regiments of United States Volunteers.[1] On May 1, 1863, Major General Nathaniel P. Banks proposed the creation of a Corps d'Afrique, embracing all the colored troops in the

Department of the Gulf. Banks envisioned a corps ultimately consisting of eighteen regiments. Believing that the lack of a military tradition among the recruits would necessitate closer-than-usual attention to instruction and training on the part of the officers, Banks limited the initial size of the regiments to five hundred men, half the traditional number.[2] He retained the right to increase the size, but in fact the colored regiments remained small until after the war.[3]

On June 6, 1863, Banks ordered the organization of the new corps. The Louisiana Native Guards, which included a recently-organized fourth regiment, became the First through Fourth Regiments of the Corps d'Afrique. A regiment then being organized in the District of Pensacola would be the Fifth Regiment. The First through Fifth Regiments of United States Volunteers, the Ullmann Brigade, became the Sixth through Tenth Regiments of the Corps d'Afrique.[4]

The tremendous increase in the number of black men and organizations in the Union army induced the War Department in 1863 to create the Bureau of Colored Troops to oversee the recruitment, organization, and command of black regiments and to establish a consistent system of designation.[5] On April 4, 1864, the War Department ordered that all black regiments be known as United States Colored Troops, abbreviated U.S.C.T. (The infantry regiments were sometimes referred to as U.S.C.I.) The regiments that had once been the Louisiana Native Guards now became the Seventy-third through Seventy-sixth U.S.C.T. The old Ullmann Brigade was renamed the Seventy-eighth through Eighty-second U.S.C.T.[6] Cyrus Hamlin's regiment thus went from being the Third United States Volunteers to the Eighth Regiment of the Corps d'Afrique to the Eightieth U.S.C.T.

The sources used to identify individuals mentioned in Hamlin's letters often employ anachronistic designations for the regiments in which those men served. For example, according to the American Civil War Research Database, John A. Nelson was commissioned into the Seventy-third U.S.C.T. in 1862. However, the War Department did not create the U.S.C.T. designation until 1864. In 1862, Nelson belonged to the First Louisiana Native Guards, which, after a time as the First Regiment of the Corps d'Afrique, became the Seventy-third U.S.C.T.

Some of the identifying information below retains these anachronistic designations. For readers interested in knowing the technically correct names of Ullmann's regiments, the following table shows the changes in their designations.

First U.S.V.	Sixth Corps d'Afrique	Seventy-eighth U.S.C.T.
Second U.S.V.	Seventh Corps d'Afrique	Seventy-ninth U.S.C.T.
Third U.S.V.	Eighth Corps d'Afrique	Eightieth U.S.C.T.

Fourth U.S.V.   Ninth Corps d'Afrique   Eighty-first U.S.C.T.
Fifth U.S.V.   Tenth Corps d'Afrique   Eighty-second U.S.C.T.

Individuals Mentioned in the Letters

Andrew, John A. (1818-1867), was an antislavery lawyer, governor of Massachusetts during the Civil War, and advocate of using black soldiers in the Union army.

Andrews, George L. (1828-1899), had seen action in Virginia and Maryland before being promoted to brigadier general in November 1862. He was Banks's chief of staff in Louisiana, accepted the surrender of Port Hudson, and briefly commanded the District of Baton Rouge and Port Hudson in late 1864 and early 1865.

Appleton, John F. (1838-1870), the son of Maine's chief justice and a captain in the Twelfth Maine Volunteers, would be colonel of the Fourth Regiment of the Ullmann Brigade (Eighty-first U.S.C.T.) from June 1863 until his resignation in July 1864. *BBGB.*

Augur, Christopher C. (1821-1898), served in the West until the Civil War. Promoted to major general of volunteers in 1862, he went to New Orleans with Banks, commanded at Baton Rouge, and led a division at Port Hudson before leaving Louisiana for the Department of Washington in October 1863. He retired from the Regular Army as a brigadier general in 1885.

Bangs, Isaac S. (1831-1903), a captain in the Twentieth Maine Infantry, joined the Ullmann Brigade as lieutenant colonel of the Fourth U.S.V. in 1863. He later served as lieutenant colonel of the Seventh U.S. Colored Artillery. In September 1863, Banks appointed him president of the examining board in New Orleans. *BBGB; CWD.*

Banks, Nathaniel P. (1816-1894), of Massachusetts was a former Speaker of the U.S. House of Representatives and a classic example of a political general. After commanding the Department of the Shenandoah, Banks replaced another political general, Benjamin F. Butler, as commander of the Department of the Gulf in December 1862. A moderate on racial issues, he released political prisoners, eased trade restrictions, and planned for escaped slaves to return to work for their old masters as sharecroppers. After leading the Port Hudson and Red River campaigns, Banks was replaced in 1864, after which he resumed his political career.

Beauregard, Pierre G. T. (1818-1893), was one of the most important Confederate generals.

Billings, Edward C. (1829-1893), a Massachusetts lawyer, moved to New Orleans in 1865, supposedly for reasons of health. He served as a federal judge in Louisiana from 1876 until his death in 1893. *DLB; New York Times*, December 2, 1893.

Blenker, Louis (Ludwig) (1812-1863), had been a wine merchant in Germany and a participant in the revolution of 1848. At the outbreak of the war, he raised a regiment of New York Germans, the Eighth New York Volunteers, and was promoted from colonel to brigadier general for his capable performance at Bull Run. He commanded a German division under Frémont in western Virginia.

Boggs, Biddle (1822-1886), an employee, friend, and business associate of Frémont, enlisted as a first lieutenant in Frémont's Mountain Department, fought at Cross Keys, joined the Eightieth U.S.C.T. as a second lieutenant, and later served as first lieutenant and quartermaster. Pamela Herr and Mary Lee Spence, eds., *The Letters of Jessie Benton Frémont* (Urbana: University of Illinois Press, 1993), 327; Paul Kens, "John C. Frémont and *The Biddle-Boggs Case*: Property Rights versus Mining Rights in Early California," *Mining History Journal* 5 (1998): 8-21; *OAR*, 257.

Botsford, Alban B. (1823-1895), a captain in the Seventy-eighth New York Volunteers, joined the Ullmann Brigade as colonel of the First Regiment. He resigned in September 1863 to be a surgeon at an army hospital in New Orleans (or, according to Bangs, to go into cotton speculation). "UB", 293; *CWD*; Albert Baxter, *History of the City of Grand Rapids, Michigan* (New York: Munsell, 1893), 719-20; *Medical Current* 11 (June 1895): 309-10.

Breckinridge, John C. (1821-1875), former U.S. vice president and the presidential candidate of southern Democrats in 1860, served the Confederacy as a major general and secretary of war.

Bridges, Charles (1838?-?), enlisted as a corporal in the Second Maine Infantry in 1861, rose to sergeant later that year, and in 1863 became first lieutenant and quartermaster, and in 1865 captain, for Cyrus Hamlin in the Third U.S.V. (Eightieth U.S.C.T.). *CWD*.

Bridges, John, was a politician and a friend and political supporter of Hannibal Hamlin. George Augustus Wheeler, *History of Castine, Penobscot, and Brooksville, Maine; including the Ancient Settlement of Pentagöet* (Bangor: Burr & Robinson, 1875), 381-82; *L&T*, 2:340.

Brown. Possibly Samuel P. Brown, a businessman of Orland, Maine, whose appointment as a civilian navy agent Hannibal Hamlin secured in 1861. Brown founded Mount Pleasant in the District of Columbia. *L&T*, 2:496; *Senate Executive Journal*, 37th Cong., 1st sess., July 27, 1861, 487; Cultural Tourism DC, "Village in the City: Mount Pleasant Heritage Trail" (Washington, D.C.: Cultural Tour-

ism DC, 2006), http://www.Culturaltourismdc.org/ usr_doc/344431_
MP_ eng _SPRD .pdf).

Buell, Don Carlos (1818-1898), was a Union major general.

Butler, Benjamin F. (1818-1893), a prominent Massachusetts lawyer and
politician who opposed slavery but still sympathized with the southern wing of the Democratic party, was a general in the state militia
when the Civil War erupted. The war turned him into a radical. Appointed major general by Lincoln, he refused to return escaped
slaves, calling them "contraband of war." With a brigade he recruited
in New England, Butler occupied New Orleans in April 1862. He
dealt forcefully with Confederate sympathizers in the city and
looked the other way when fellow northerners profited improperly
from their positions as occupiers. Recalled in December 1862, Butler
later served without distinction in the East and resumed his political
career after the war.

Cailloux, Andre (1825-1863), was a free, Paris-educated black man and
cigar maker of New Orleans and a captain in the First Louisiana Native Guards. He died leading his men in the assault on Port Hudson
on May 27, 1863. *DLB* (named misspelled as Callioux); James G.
Hollandsworth, Jr., *The Louisiana Native Guards: The Black Military Experience During the Civil War* (Baton Rouge: Louisiana State
University Press, 1995), 27, 54-55.

Canby, Edward R. S. (1817-1873), a career soldier, was given command
of the Department of New Mexico in 1861. Promoted to brigadier
general in 1862 and major general in 1864, he assumed command of
the Military Division of West Mississippi, which included the Department of the Gulf, in 1864.

Cantrell, Joseph, enlisted in the Seventh New York National Guard as a
private. In February 1863, he joined the Third U.S.V. as a second
lieutenant, and in December 1863 was promoted to first lieutenant in
the Eightieth U.S.C.T. He resigned in 1864. *CWD*; William Swinton,
*History of the Seventh Regiment, National Guard, State of New York,
During the War of the Rebellion* (New York: Fields, Osgood, 1870),
255, 424.

Carter, William S. (1826?-1863), enlisted in 1862 as a sergeant in
Charles Hamlin's regiment, the Eighteenth Maine Infantry, transferred to the First Maine Heavy Artillery, and joined Cyrus's regiment as first lieutenant in June 1863. He died of disease in July 1863.
CWD; *OAR*, 257.

Casey, Silas (1807-1882), a Union general, authored a manual on infantry tactics. The army published a version written especially for colored troops in 1863.

Chase, Salmon P. (1808-1873), a leader in the antislavery cause and former governor of Ohio and U.S. senator, was secretary of the treasury from 1861 to 1864 and chief justice of the United States from 1864 until his death.

Clapp, William H. (1828-1904), was a captain and assistant adjutant general for Major General Francis J. Herron, who in 1865 commanded the Northern Division of Louisiana, headquartered at Baton Rouge. *CWD*; *MR*, 275.

Clark, James C. (1818?-1864), enlisted as a captain in 1861 in Troy, New York, at the age of forty-three. He was commissioned into the U.S.V. Adjutant General Department as captain and assistant adjutant general in May 1862 and joined Ullmann's Brigade as a lieutenant colonel, Second U.S.V., in February 1863. Promoted to colonel on July 12, 1863, Clark died of disease in September 1864. *CWD*.

Cluseret, Gustave P. (1823-1900), a French military officer and adventurer, came to the United States in 1862 and served Major General George B. McClellan and then Frémont as a staff officer. Frémont put Colonel Cluseret in command of a light brigade.

Conway, Thomas W. (1839?-1887), formerly chaplain of the Ninth New York Volunteers, was the assistant commissioner of the Freedmen's Bureau for Louisiana. President Johnson replaced Conway in September 1865. Although it is generally held that Johnson removed Conway because of the latter's radicalism, Hamlin may have felt that Conway was not radical enough. See Caryn Cossé Bell, "'Une Chimère': The Freedmen's Bureau in Creole New Orleans," in *The Freedmen's Bureau and Reconstruction: Reconsiderations*, ed. Paul A. Cimbala and Randall M. Miller (New York: Fordham University Press, 1999), 140-60; *Brooklyn Eagle*, April 7, 1887, April 8, 1887.

Davis, Jefferson (1808-1889), former U.S. senator and secretary of war, was president of the Confederate States of America.

Deering, Nathaniel C. (1827-1887), was a Maine state legislator in 1855-1856 and friend of Hannibal Hamlin. He served as a clerk in the U.S. Senate during the Civil War and later as a congressman from Iowa. *L&T*, 2:317.

Denison, George S. (1833-1866), was a special agent for the U.S. Treasury Department, acting collector of customs, and then acting collector of internal revenue in New Orleans during the Civil War. James A. Padgett, ed., "Some Letters of George Stanton Denison, 1854-1866," *Louisiana Historical Quarterly* 23 (October 1940): 1132-38.

Des Anges, Robert A. (d. 1894), born in England, was a soldier of fortune who fought in India and the Crimea before the Civil War. He enlisted as a captain in the Ninth Regiment of the Corp d'Afrique in 1863. In 1864, he was promoted to major and appointed assistant adjutant-general for Ullmann. Des Anges subsequently held the same position under Brigadier General Edward R. C. Canby. "UB", 298; *CWD.*

Dickey, William H. (1840-1902), began the war as a sergeant in the Sixth Michigan Infantry. After promotion to first lieutenant, Dickey became colonel of the Twelfth Regiment, Corps d'Afrique (Eighty-fourth U.S.C.T.) in 1863. *BBGB; CWD.*

Dostie, Anthony Paul (1821-1866), was a New-York-born dentist who moved to New Orleans around mid-century. He vigorously opposed secession, fled New Orleans in 1861, and returned after Federal troops occupied the city. He remained an outspoken Unionist and radical advocate of civil rights and suffrage for blacks. Wounded in the riot of July 30, 1866, he died a few days later. *DLB.*

Drew, Charles W. (1835-1903), enlisted in 1861 as a first lieutenant in the Seventy-fifth New York Infantry. He later became colonel of the Seventy-sixth U.S.C.T. and appears to have succeeded Cyrus in command of the First Division of the Corps d'Afrique around the middle of 1864. Drew led a brigade of black soldiers in the Mobile campaign of 1865. *BBGB; OR,* ser. 1, vol. 34, pt. 4, p. 613.

Dudley, Nathan A. M. (1825-1910), was the colonel in command of the Third Brigade, First Division, Nineteenth Army Corps in Louisiana in May 1863, when Cyrus mentions him in a letter. *BBGB; MR,* 302-03; Robert M. Utley, *High Noon in Lincoln: Violence on the Western Frontier* (Albuquerque: University of New Mexico Press, 1987), 66 and *passim.*

Durant, Thomas J. (1817-1882), moved as a teenager from his native Philadelphia to New Orleans, where he became a publisher, lawyer, and Democratic politician. During the Civil War, he turned against slavery and towards radical reconstruction. After the New Orleans race riot of 1866, Durant departed Louisiana for Washington, D.C., where he enjoyed a successful legal practice.

Durell, Edward H. (1810-1887), a native of New Hampshire, moved to New Orleans in 1837 and there developed a thriving law practice. A Union Democrat, he headed the New Orleans Bureau of Finance, was acting military mayor in 1863, and served as a federal judge in Louisiana from 1863 until 1874.

Dwight, William (1831-1888), a Union brigadier general, participated in the attack on Port Hudson in 1863 and served as Banks's chief of staff in 1864 before being reassigned to the eastern theater.

Emerson, Levi (1816?-?), a former police officer and political supporter of Hannibal Hamlin, enlisted in Bangor as a captain in the Second Maine Infantry in 1861. He was discharged for disability on October 22, 1862. *L&T,* 2:407; *CWD.*

Farley. There was a Charles H. Farley in Portland who was the grand-nephew of Hannibal Hamlin's cousin, Dr. Cyrus Hamlin, a well-known missionary. Cyrus mentions him in connection with the Carmick and Ramsay claim, but what Farley had to do with the case is unknown.

Fessenden, Samuel (1841?-1862), a son of William Pitt Fessenden, enlisted as a second lieutenant in the Maine Second Light Artillery Battery in 1861, was promoted to first lieutenant, and was mortally wounded at Second Bull Run in August 1862. *CWD.*

Fessenden, Thomas A. D. (1826-1868), a brother of William Pitt Fessenden, was a lawyer who served several terms in the Maine legislature and for three months in 1857-1858 finished out the unexpired term of a deceased U.S. senator.

Fiske, William O. (1838-1886), was a first lieutenant and aide on Butler's staff who rose to captain in the Thirty-first Massachusetts Infantry, then major (1862) and colonel (1863) in the First Louisiana (Union) Infantry. *BBGB; CWD.*

Flanders, Benjamin F. (1816-1896), a native of New Hampshire, moved to New Orleans in 1843. There he engaged in local politics and worked as a railroad company executive. He served a few months in Congress as a Unionist in 1862-1863 and ran unsuccessfully for governor of Louisiana in 1864. After the Civil War, he remained active in local government, serving as military governor of Louisiana and mayor of New Orleans.

Frémont, Jessie Benton (1804-1902), the daughter of influential U.S. senator Thomas Hart Benton, married John C. Frémont in 1841. Politically savvy, she actively promoted her husband's political and military career.

Frémont, John C. (1813-1890) was already famous as an army surveyor and explorer in America's western wilderness and as the first Republican presidential nominee when the Civil War erupted. He was appointed major general commanding the Department of the West. In 1861, Frémont issued a decree emancipating the slaves of Missouri rebels, but Lincoln compelled him to rescind the decree and soon afterwards relieved him of command. Placed in charge of Union forces in western Virginia in 1862, Frémont resigned after the reorganization of his command. His military career over, he dabbled in politics during the war and afterwards engaged unsuccessfully in business.

Getchell, Marshall P. (1837- 1902), enlisted in the Ninth Maine Infantry as sergeant major in 1861, resigned due to illness, recovered, and enlisted in the Eightieth U.S.C.T. He resigned as a first lieutenant and adjutant in August 1863. *CWD*; Emma Siggins White, comp.,

The Kinnears and Their Kin (Kansas City, Mo.: Tiernan-Dart, 1916), 124-25; *OAR*, 257.

Ghyka, Eugene, supposedly a Moldavian prince, was a captain in Zu-lavsky's regiment, the Fifth Regiment (Eighty-second U.S.C.T.) of Ullmann's brigade. He returned to Moldavia in the fall of 1863 and later commanded a division in the Russo-Turkish War of 1877-1878. "UB", 301.

Gober, Daniel C. (1828-1889), was, in May 1865, the Confederate colo-nel in command of the District of Southwest Mississippi and East Louisiana. Bruce S. Allardice, *Confederate Colonels: A Biographi-cal Register* (Columbia: University of Missouri Press, 2008), 165-66.

Godfrey, John E. (1809-1884), was a lawyer and judge in Bangor, Maine. In the 1840s he edited an antislavery newspaper. Albert Ware Paine, "John E. Godfrey," in *Collections and Proceedings of the Maine Historical Society*, 2nd ser., 1 (1890): 79-85.

Godfrey, John F. (1839-1885), the son of John E. Godfrey, enlisted in 1861 as a second lieutenant in the First Maine Mounted Battery. In 1862, he raised a company for the First Louisiana Cavalry, of which he became captain, and in 1863 became lieutenant colonel of the Second Maine Cavalry. He resigned due to poor health in 1864. *CWD*; William E. S. Whitman and Charles H. True, *Maine in the War for the Union: A History of the Part Borne by Maine Troops in the Suppression of the American Rebellion* (Lewiston, Me.: Nelson Dingley Jr., 1865), 385, 563; Candace Sawyer and Laura Orcutt, eds., *The Civil War Letters of Capt. John Franklin Godfrey* (South Port-land, Me.: Ascensius Press, 1993), Introduction (unpaginated), 14, 16, 35, 70-71.

Golden. A general order issued by Brigadier General Egbert Brown in Missouri in 1863 refers to "Captain Golden, Government horse-dealer." Frank Moore, ed., *The Rebellion Record: A Diary of Ameri-can Events, with Documents, Narratives, Illustrative Incidents, Po-etry, etc.*, vol. 7 (New York: D. Van Nostrand, 1864), 77 (Poetry and Incidents section).

Goodloe, John K., was a lawyer and politician from Versailles, Kentucky. He was confirmed as U.S. district attorney for the Eastern District of Louisiana on February 15, 1866, and subsequently dismissed from the position by President Johnson. *Senate Executive Journal*, 39th Cong., 1st sess., February 16, 1866, 561.

Gregory, Edgar M. (1804-1871), a staunch abolitionist, was brevetted brigadier general in 1864 and major general in 1865. At the end of the war, Gregory was appointed assistant commissioner of the Freedmen's Bureau for Texas, a position he held until April 1866. *BBGB*; *CWD*; Roy R. Barkley, ed., *The Handbook of Texas Online*

(Denton, Tex.: Texas State Historical Association), http://www.tshaonline.org/handbook/online/ articles/GG/fgr52.html.

Griffith, John (1831-1889), was colonel of the Confederate Consolidated (Eleventh and Seventeenth) Arkansas Infantry (mounted). Bruce S. Allardice, *Confederate Colonels: A Biographical Register* (Columbia: University of Missouri Press, 2008), 174-75.

Hahn, Michael D. (1830-1866), born in Germany, moved in 1840 to New Orleans, where he later became a lawyer and Unionist Democrat. After the Union army occupied New Orleans, Hahn was elected congressman in 1862, governor in 1864, and U.S. senator in 1865. He refused to take his Senate seat in protest of President Johnson's Reconstruction policy. Hahn was wounded in the New Orleans race riot of 1866. In 1867, he founded the *New Orleans Republican*. He remained active in state politics after the war.

Hall, James Abram (1835-1893), enlisted as a first lieutenant in the Maine Second Light Artillery Battery in 1861, was promoted to captain in May 1861, and ended the war as a lieutenant colonel and brevet brigadier general. *CWD.*

Halsted, George B. (1820-?), was assistant adjutant general under Major General Christopher C. Augur and Brigadier General George L. Andrews. William S. Stryker, *Record of Officers and Men of New Jersey in the Civil War, 1861-1865* (Trenton: John L. Murphy, 1876), 1:11; William H. Shaw, comp., *History of Essex and Hudson Counties, New Jersey* (Philadelphia: Evarts & Peck, 1884), 1:280.

Hamlin, Augustus C. (1829-1905), the son of Hannibal Hamlin's brother Elijah, studied medicine at Harvard and in Paris, joined the Second Maine Infantry as assistant surgeon in 1861, served with Frémont in the Shenandoah Valley, and subsequently was promoted to lieutenant colonel and medical inspector and ultimately to medical inspector-general of the Army of the Tennessee. Mustered out in October 1865, he returned to Bangor as a doctor and writer on medical and other topics. *CWD*; *MR*, 77-78; *Obituary Record of the Graduates of Bowdoin College and the Medical School of Maine for the Decade Ending 1 June 1909* (Brunswick, Me.: Bowdoin College Library, 1911), 340-41.

Hamlin, Charles (1837-1911), Cyrus Hamlin's brother, was a lawyer who served as a recruiting officer in Maine early in the war. Commissioned major in the Eighteenth Maine Volunteers in 1862, he saw action at Gettysburg and elsewhere. Hamlin was brevetted brigadier general in 1865. He resigned from the army that year, but remained active in veterans' affairs.

Hamlin, Joshua Gamage (1836?-1865), a distant relative of Cyrus Hamlin, enlisted in Sweden, Maine, in 1861 as a private in the Fifth

Maine Infantry. He transferred to the Third U.S.V. as a first lieutenant in June 1863 and was promoted to captain in 1865. He died of
disease on August 12, 1865. *CWD*; *OAR*, 257.

Hapgood. Probably Second Lieutenant John H. Hapgood (1842-?) of the
Fourth Massachusetts Light Artillery Battery, which spent most of
its existence in Louisiana. He either was promoted to first lieutenant
in his battery or resigned and joined the Second Louisiana Infantry
(Union), organized in New Orleans, as a first lieutenant. *CWD*; *Utica
Morning Herald*, November 5, 1887.

Harris, Ira (1802-1875), was a Republican U.S. senator from 1861 to
1867.

Hatch, Joseph H., a private in the Twentieth Maine Infantry, joined the
Eightieth U.S.C.T. as a second lieutenant, but resigned on August 25,
1863. *OAR*, 257.

Hatch, William A. (1841?-?), enlisted as a second lieutenant in the Third
Maine Infantry in 1861 and was promoted to first lieutenant later
that year and to captain in 1862. He was discharged in March 1863
and enlisted as a major in the Third U.S.V. He resigned in March
1865. *CWD*; *OAR*, 257.

Hawkins, John P. (1830-1914), promoted to brigadier general in command of the District of Northeast Louisiana in 1863, commanded the
First Division of U.S.C.T. in 1864 and 1865.

Hersey, Samuel Freeman (1812-1875), one of Maine's leading lumber-
men, was a friend and political associate of Hannibal Hamlin. He
was active in state government from the 1840s through the 1860s
and served as a Republican in the U.S. House of Representatives
from 1873 until his death.

Hichborn, Nathan G. (?-1874), was a shipbuilder and Republican politician from Waldo County, Maine, who served as state treasurer from
1865 to 1868. Faustina Hichborn, *Historical Sketch of Stockton
Springs*, ed. Herbert C. Libby (Waterville, Me.: Central Maine Pub.
Co., 1908), 20-23, 34, 39.

Hill was either Albert G. Hills (1829?-1879), a reporter for the *Boston
Journal*, or Alfred C. Hills, a reporter for the *New York Evening Post*
and other papers. A. C. Hills was lieutenant colonel and A. G. Hills
first lieutenant of the Fourth Louisiana Native Guards in March 1863,
when Banks installed them as editors of the *New Orleans Era*, formerly the *Daily Delta*, in order to have a pro-Union voice in the
city's press. The *Era* folded in January 1865. *OAR*, 252; Senate
Committee on Claims, 47th Cong., 1st sess., 1882, S. Rep. 786; *Lit-
erary World*, 10 (July 5,1879): 222-23.

Hodsdon. John L. (1815-1895), a lawyer and militia officer, was adjutant
general of Maine during the Civil War. *Maine Farmer*, March 7,

1895; Kenneth E. Thompson, *Civil War Maine Hall of Fame: Political, Judicial, and Military Leaders, 1861-1865* (Portland, Me.: Thompson Group, 2000), 15.

Hopper, John C., captain, was an additional aide-de-camp to Frémont and his chief of scouts and spies. William S. Stryker, *Record of Officers and Men of New Jersey in the Civil War, 1861-1865* (Trenton: John L. Murphy, 1876), 1:11; *OR*, ser. 1, vol. 12, pt. 1, p. 35.

Howard, Oliver O. (1830-1909), a native of Maine, was promoted to major general in 1862. In 1865, President Johnson appointed him the first commissioner of the Freedmen's Bureau.

Howell, Rufus K., was a Unionist judge in New Orleans who kept his district court open when other judges refused to operate during the Federal takeover of the city. He joined the Louisiana Supreme Court in 1865 and served as president of the 1866 Louisiana constitutional convention. *DLB*; Thomas W. Helis, "Of Generals and Jurists: The Judicial System of New Orleans under Union Occupation, May 1862—April 1865," in *A Law Unto Itself? Essays in the New Louisiana Legal History*, ed. Warren M. Billings and Mark Fernandez (Baton Rouge: Louisiana State University Press, 2001).

Hughes, Augustus De Berkeley (1834-1875), was Edward C. Billings's law partner in New York. He accompanied Billings to New Orleans, where the two men joined with James P. Sullivan to form Sullivan, Billings & Hughes. For about six months in 1863, Hughes was a judge of the Louisiana provost court, a court of criminal jurisdiction established by the military authorities. *New York Times*, December 2, 1893; *Obituary Record of Graduates of Yale College Deceased from June, 1870, to June, 1880* (New Haven: Tuttle, Morehouse & Taylor, 1880), 190; Charles Gardner, comp., *Gardner's New Orleans Directory for 1867* (New Orleans: Charles Gardner, 1867), 209; Henry N. Cobb, *Decennial Report of the Class of 1855, of Yale College* (New York: Alfred Cobb, 1866), 72.

Hunter, David (1802-1886), commanded the Department of the West before being placed in charge of the Department of the South in March 1862. On May 9, 1862, Hunter ordered the abolition of slavery in his department, an action quickly reversed by President Lincoln.

Jackson, Thomas J. "Stonewall" (1824-1863), a graduate of the United States Military Academy, veteran of the Mexican War, and instructor at the Virginia Military Institute, gained his greatest fame for the Shenandoah Valley campaign, when he was a major general. At the time of his death from "friendly fire," he held the rank of lieutenant general.

Johnson, Andrew (1808-1875), the only U.S. senator from the seceding states who refused to vacate his seat, was chosen to replace Hannibal Hamlin as Lincoln's running mate in 1864 in an appeal to War Democrats. Johnson became president upon Lincoln's assassination in 1865.

Johnson, Edward (1816-1873) was a Confederate brigadier general who was badly wounded at McDowell.

Jones, Samuel B. (1826-1908), enlisted in 1861 as a captain in the Seventy-eighth New York Infantry. In February 1863 he joined the Ullmann Brigade as lieutenant colonel of the First Regiment, but soon replaced Alban Botsford as colonel. *BBGB; CWD.*

Jones, William Hemphill (1811-1880), was chief clerk in the office of the First Comptroller of the U.S. Treasury at the time of Elisha Whittlesey's death in 1863. *Obituary Record of Graduates of Yale College Deceased from June, 1870, to June, 1880* (New Haven: Tuttle, Morehouse & Taylor, 1880), 390-91.

Kimball, William King (1820-1875), enlisted as lieutenant colonel of the Twelfth Maine Infantry in November 1861, and became colonel of the regiment in July 1862. *BBGB; CWD.*

King, Preston (1805-1865) was a Republican U.S. senator from 1857 to 1863.

Kirby Smith, Edmund (1824-1893), Confederate lieutenant general, was given command of the Trans-Mississippi Department in 1863. On May 26, 1865, he surrendered the last significant Confederate army.

Lane. Lane is probably James Henry Lane (1814-1866), a Radical Republican U.S. senator from Kansas during the Civil War. However, Cyrus could have been referring to Henry Smith Lane (1811-1881), a moderate Republican from Indiana, who sat in the Senate at the same time.

Lawler, Michael K. (1814-1882), a brigadier general, held commands in the Departments of the Tennessee and the Gulf.

Lee, Robert E. (1807-1870), Confederate general, had command of Virginia's military forces and served as military advisor to Confederate president Jefferson Davis early in the war. In June 1862, he assumed command of the Army of Northern Virginia.

Lincoln, Abraham (1809-1865), took office as the first Republican U.S. president in 1861 and was mortally wounded by an assassin on April 14, 1865.

Lipscomb. Possibly Confederate captain Albert A. Lipscomb (1834-1869) of the Twentieth Louisiana Infantry. After several consolidations and reorganizations, the Twentieth ended up as part of the Pelican Consolidated Infantry Regiment (April-May, 1865) in the Department of Alabama, Mississippi, and East Louisiana. The Civil War Database does not list Lipscomb on its roster of the Pelican Regiment's personnel. Find a Grave, http://www.findagrave.com; Stewart Sifakis, *Compendium of the Confederate Armies: Louisiana* (Westminster, Md.: Willow Bend Books, 2007), 106-07, 128; *CWD*.

Long, Alanson B. (1837-1870), enlisted in Greenfield, Massachusetts, and was commissioned a captain in the Fifty-second Massachusetts Infantry. He was mustered out in August 1863. After the war he practiced law in New Orleans, and in 1870 was United States attorney for Louisiana. *CWD*; Charles Gardner, comp., *Gardner's New Orleans Directory for 1867* (New Orleans: Charles Gardner, 1867), 252; *Senate Executive Journal*, 41st Cong., 2nd sess., April 13, 1870, 424, and 3rd sess., December 8, 1870, 554.

Lynde, John H. (1827-1874), published the *Bangor Daily Whig and Courier* with William H. Wheeler. Joseph Griffin, ed., *History of the Press of Maine* (Brunswick, Me.: Press of J. Griffin, 1872), 133.

Manning, Elbridge G. (1843?-1869), enlisted as a corporal in the Nineteenth Massachusetts Infantry in 1861. In February 1863, he joined the Ullmann Brigade as first lieutenant and adjutant in the Fourth U.S.V. A captain when his regiment was mustered out in 1866, Manning joined the Fifth U.S. Infantry as a second lieutenant in 1867 and stayed in service until his death. *CWD*; *MR*, 383-84.

Mayo, Ezekiel R. (1834?-?), entered the service as first lieutenant of the Maine Third Light Artillery Battery in 1861, transferred to the Maine First Heavy Artillery, and then transferred back to the Third Light Artillery. At some point, he was promoted to captain. *CWD.*

Mayo. Possibly Gideon Mayo (1808-1876) of Orono, Maine, a businessman, politician, and militia officer who in the fall of 1862 was named draft commissioner for Penobscot County. William Richard Cutter, ed., *New England Families: Genealogical and Memorial* (New York: Lewis Historical Pub. Co., 1914), 3:1625; William E. S. Whitman and Charles H. True, *Maine in the War for the Union: A History of the Part Borne by Maine Troops in the Suppression of the American Rebellion* (Lewiston, Me.: Nelson Dingley Jr., 1865), 10. Mayo could also be Ezekiel R. Mayo of Hampden, Maine (see above).

McFadden, Orrin, was teaching school in Georgia when the war broke out. He joined a Georgia regiment, escaped to the Union lines, and was mustered in as a Federal soldier in 1863. A captain in Cyrus's regiment, the Eightieth U.S.C.T., he was discharged as a lieutenant colonel in 1867. Charles E. Allen, "Some Huguenots and Other Early Settlers on the Kennebec in Dresden," in *Collections and Proceedings of the Maine Historical Society*, 2nd ser., 3 (1892): 377.

McNeil, John (1813-1891), a Union brigadier general, served the entire war in Missouri.

Merrill, James F. (1837-1917), a native of Maine, enlisted as a sergeant in the Seventh Rhode Island Volunteers in 1862 and was promoted to first lieutenant in July 1863. William P. Hopkins, *The Seventh Regiment, Rhode Island Volunteers, in the Civil War, 1862-1865* (Providence: Providence Press, 1903), 363-64; *CWD.*

Milroy, Robert H. (1816-1890), brigadier general, fought a fierce campaign against guerillas in western Virginia in 1862, which led to his promotion to major general in 1863.

Monroe, John T. (1823-1871), a Virginia-born former stevedore and labor leader, was elected mayor of New Orleans in 1860. His failure to cooperate with Union military authorities led to his arrest and imprisonment in 1862. Released in 1863, he sat out the rest of the war in Mobile, Alabama. Reelected mayor of New Orleans in 1865, Monroe received much of the blame for the 1866 race riot. Sheridan removed him from office again in 1867. *DLB.*

Moore, William C. (1832?-?), enlisted in 1862 as a sergeant in the Eighteenth Maine Infantry, transferred to the First Maine Heavy Artillery, and joined Cyrus's regiment as second lieutenant in June 1863. He resigned in August 1863. *CWD*; *OAR*, 257.

Morrill, Lot M. (1813-1883), was a Republican U.S. senator from Maine from 1861 to 1876 and later secretary of the treasury.

Morse, Ruggles Sylvester (1815-1893), was a native of Maine who by the 1850s was a wealthy hotelier in New Orleans. Arthur Douglas Stover, comp., *Eminent Mainers: Succinct Biographies of Thousands of Amazing Mainers, Mostly Dead, and a Few People from Away Who Have Done Something Useful Within the State of Maine* (Gardiner, Me.: Tilbury House, 2006), 345.

Mudgett, Benjamin F. (1822-1886), a lawyer from Bangor, Maine, moved to New York City in 1856 and served as deputy collector in the New York customs house from 1862 to 1867. Percy Leroy Ricker and Elwin R. Holland, *A Genealogy of the Ricker Family* (Westminster, Md.: Heritage Books, 1996), 1:82; George Adams, *The Maine Register, and Business Directory, for the Year 1856* (South Berwick, Me.: Edward C. Parks, [1856?]), 206; Senate Committee of Investigation and Retrenchment, *Report and Testimony of the Committee on Investigation and Retrenchment, on Alleged Frauds in the New York Custom-House*, 42d Cong., 2d sess., 1872, S. Rep. 227, 452.

Mudgett, Lewis P. (1836?-1865), brother of William S. Mudgett, from Stockton, Maine, enlisted as a private in the Second Maine Infantry in 1861, received promotions to sergeant major in 1861, first lieutenant and adjutant, and then captain in 1862. He was mustered out in 1863, but subsequently served as a captain in Cyrus Hamlin's regiment, the Eightieth U.S.C.T., and a major in the Eighty-sixth U.S.C.T. He was killed in action on April 9, 1865. *CWD*; *OAR*, 266.

Mudgett, William S. (1837-1899), brother of Lewis P. Mudgett, enlisted as a private in the Second Maine Infantry in 1861. He was mustered out as a captain in 1863, then joined Cyrus's regiment, the Third Regiment of the Ullmann Brigade, as lieutenant colonel a few months later. He succeeded Cyrus as colonel of the Eightieth U.S.C.T. Bangs remembered him as "a brave and accomplished officer." After the war, Mudgett remained in Louisiana as a politician and cotton planter. *BBGB*; *CWD*; "UB", 294.

Nelson, John A. (1834?-?) enlisted as a captain in the Thirtieth Massachusetts Infantry. Mustered out in 1862, he enlisted in the Seventy-third U.S.C.T. as lieutenant colonel and was promoted to colonel of the Seventy-fifth U.S.C.T. Nelson resigned in August 1863, but later that year was commissioned colonel of the Tenth U.S.C.T. in Virginia. *CWD*.

Nickerson, Franklin S. (1826-1917), was colonel of the Fourteenth Maine Infantry, serving in the Department of the Gulf. He was promoted to brigadier general in 1863.

Nye, Watson (1843-?), enlisted in the Twelfth Maine Infantry in 1861 and appears to have been promoted to second lieutenant in the U.S.C.T. in June 1863. He was still living as of 1930. *CWD*; George Barbour, "Some Civil War Soldiers of Northwestern Maine (M-Z)," http://www.geocities.com/ barbour/1028/CWSoldiersM-Z.htm).

Nye, William E., a captain in the Eightieth U.S.C.T., was later promoted to lieutenant colonel in the Seventy-sixth U.S.C.T. *OAR*, 252, 257.

Pickard. Probably Amos Pickard (1815-1880) of Hampden, Maine, a state legislator and political supporter of Hannibal Hamlin. *L&T*, 2:245, 340; Mike Desmarais, transcriptions from Lakeview Cemetery, Hampden, Maine, USGenWeb Archives, http://files.usgwarchives.org/me/penobscot/hampden /cemetery/lakeview.txt.

Pile, William A. (1829-1889), a brigadier general, commanded a black brigade in St. Louis. He was brevetted major general in 1865 for his command of a black division in the campaign against Mobile.

Plaisted, James H. (1833?-?), enlisted with the Third Maine Infantry as a sergeant-major in 1861 and was made captain three days later. At the time of his resignation from the army on October 3, 1863, he was first lieutenant and quartermaster of the Eightieth U.S.C.T. *CWD*; *OAR*, 257.

Plumly, B. Rush (1816-1887), was an abolitionist from Philadelphia whom Banks appointed in 1863 to a commission to regulate the recruitment and enrollment of troops for the Corps d'Afrique and in 1864 to chair the Board of Education for Freedmen in the Department of the Gulf. James M. McPherson, *The Struggle for Equality: Abolitionists and the Negro in the Civil War and Reconstruction* (Princeton: Princeton University Press, 1964), 208, 291-93.

Pope, John (1822-1892), a major general, commanded the Army of Virginia briefly in 1862 and then the Department of the Northwest.

Reed, S. Tyler, was captain of an unattached cavalry company that Banks eventually attached to the Third Massachusetts Cavalry. He served under Butler during the expedition against New Orleans in 1862 and at Port Hudson in 1863. Reed was promoted to major in 1863. Frederick W. Coburn, *History of Lowell and Its People* (New York: Lewis Historical Pub. Co., 1920), 1:323; James K. Ewer, *The Third Massachusetts Cavalry in the War for the Union* (Maplewood, Mass.: Wm. G. J. Perry, 1903), 99, 110-11.

Reeve, Isaac V. D. (1813-1890), lieutenant colonel, was chief mustering and disbursing officer in New York City. *BBGB*; George W. Cullem, *Biographical Register of the Officers and Graduates of the U.S. Military Academy at West Point, N. Y. from its Establishment, in 1802, to 1890 with the Early History of the United States Military Academy*, 3rd ed. (Boston: Houghton, Mifflin, 1891), 1:620-21.

Reynolds, Joseph J. (1822-1899), major general, was put in charge of the defenses of New Orleans in January 1864. In November, he replaced Major General Frederick Steele in command of the Department of Arkansas.

Rice. Possibly Albert R. Rice (1835-1923) of Springfield, Massachusetts. Enlisting as an assistant surgeon in 1862, he served first with the First Massachusetts Cavalry and then with the Forth-ninth Massachusetts Infantry. After being mustered out of the latter regiment in September 1863, Rice was commissioned into the Navy Medical Department. In July 1863, the Forty-ninth Massachusetts was in Donaldsonville, Louisiana. *CWD*.

Rice, John H. (1816-1911), was a Republican congressman from Maine during the Civil War.

Roberts. Possibly Captain Eugene F. Roberts (d. 1888) of the Eighty-second U.S.C.T. *CWD*.

Ruse. Possibly J. D. Rouse, a captain in the Seventy-seventh and then the 113th Illinois Volunteers who after the war practiced law in New Orleans with great success. Henry Clay Warmouth, *War, Politics and Reconstruction: Stormy Days in Louisiana* (New York: Macmillan, 1930), 30; W. H. Bentley, *History of the 77th Illinois Volunteer Infantry, Sept. 2, 1862, - July 10, 1865* (Peoria: Edward Hine, 1883), *passim*.

Sanborn, Sarah L. (1841?-1863), who would marry Cyrus on October 12, 1862, was the daughter of True and Sarah Sanborn of Prospect, Waldo County, Maine. H. Franklin Andrews, *The Hamlin Family: A Genealogy of James Hamlin of Barnstable Massachusetts* (Exira, Iowa: privately published, 1902), 649.

Schenk, Robert C. (1809-1890), brigadier general, commanded Frémont's right wing at the Battle of Cross Keys.

Seward, William H. (1801-1872), former governor of New York and U.S. senator, served as Lincoln's secretary of state.

Sewell. Probably Charles W. Lowell (1834-1877), of Foxcroft, Maine. A Maine state representative in 1862, Lowell joined the Eightieth U.S.C.T. as a captain in 1863 and subsequently served as a provost judge, Speaker of the Louisiana House of Representatives, and postmaster in New Orleans. Aldice G. Warren, ed. *Catalogue of the Delta Kappa Epsilon Fraternity* (New York: Δ K E Council, 1910), 227. (Some of the information presented in this source is inaccurate.)

Shaw, Alfred (1826-?), a Pennsylvania native, one-time sheriff of Orleans Parish, and delegate to the 1864 Louisiana constitutional convention and to the reassembled convention of 1866, was wounded in the New Orleans riot. *Crucible of Reconstruction: War, Radicalism and Race in Louisiana, 1862-1877* (Baton Rouge: Louisiana State University Press, 1984), 227; James G. Hollandsworth, Jr., *An Absolute Massacre: The New Orleans Race Riot of July 30, 1866* (Baton Rouge: Louisiana State University Press, 2001), 115-16.

Shields, James (1806-1879), brigadier general, fought Stonewall Jackson in the Shenandoah Valley campaign, then resigned in 1863 to resume his legal and political career.

Sheridan, Philip H. (1831-1888), gained fame in the Civil War as a cavalry and division commander. After Lee's surrender, Major General Sheridan commanded the Military Division of the Gulf. Promoted to lieutenant general in 1869, Sheridan became commanding general of the army in 1883.

Sherman, Thomas W. (1813-1879), brigadier general, after being severely wounded at Port Hudson in 1863, held administrative positions in Louisiana for the rest of the war.

Sickles, Daniel E. (1819-1914), major general, was in New Orleans in mid-1864 following a tour down the Mississippi River.

Slidell, John (1793-1871), of New Orleans served in both houses of Congress before the Civil War. In 1861, while on a diplomatic mission for the Confederacy, he was taken off a British mail steamer by the commander of U.S. naval vessel, but was eventually allowed to continue on his journey. Slidell served as the Confederate ambassador to France.

Smith, Andrew J. (1815-1897), major general, served primarily in Missouri, Kentucky, and Tennessee, but in 1865 he participated in the capture of Mobile.

Soulé, Pierre (1801-1870), a Confederate politician and diplomat from New Orleans, was captured and imprisoned by Federal forces. He made his way back to the South after being paroled and supported the Confederate cause.

Sprague. Probably William Sprague (1830-1915), U.S. senator from Rhode Island and Salmon P. Chase's son-in-law.

Stafford, Spencer H. (1822?-1888), a captain in the First Louisiana Native Guards, formerly lieutenant colonel of the Eleventh New York Infantry and then Butler's provost marshal or assistant provost marshal in New Orleans, was dismissed from the service by a court-martial in May 1863, for a tirade in which he accused other officers of stealing from and otherwise mistreating his regiment. The next year, though, he appeared as colonel of the Tenth U.S.C.T. After the war, Stafford appealed his conviction of "conduct to the prejudice of good order and military discipline" and received an honorable discharge retroactive to the date of dismissal. "The New Hartford Centennial," *Transactions of the Oneida Historical Society* (Utica, N. Y.: Ellis H. Roberts & Co., 1889), 14n; *OR*, ser. 1, vol. 36, pt. 3, p. 430; James G. Hollandsworth, Jr., *The Louisiana Native Guards: The Black Military Experience During the Civil War* (Baton Rouge: Louisiana State University Press, 1995), 49-51 and *passim*.

Stanton, Edwin M. (1814-1869), was an antislavery Democratic lawyer from Ohio who moved to Washington, D.C. in 1856. President James Buchanan appointed him attorney general in 1859, and President Lincoln named him secretary of war in 1862.

Steele, Frederick (1819-1868), major general, was given command of the Department of Arkansas in 1863.

Sullivan, James P., was a partner in the law firm of Sullivan, Billings & Hughes in the 1860s. Charles Gardner, comp., *Gardner's New Orleans Directory for 1867* (New Orleans: Charles Gardner, 1867), 379.

Sumner, Charles (1811-1874), a Massachusetts lawyer and a founder of the Free Soil Party, was an outspoken abolitionist and a Republican U.S. senator from 1851 until his death.

Taylor, Miles (1805-1873), was a native New Yorker who studied medicine and law and was admitted to the bar in Donaldsonville, Louisiana. He moved to New Orleans around 1847, and served in Congress from 1855 to 1861, after which he resumed his legal practice in New Orleans.

Thomas, Henry Goddard (1837-1897), entered the military in 1861 as a private in the Fifth Maine Infantry, but he soon became a captain and transferred at that rank to the Eleventh U.S. Infantry. Commissioned colonel of the Second U.S.V. (Seventy-ninth U.S.C.T.), Ullmann Brigade, in March 1863, Thomas took command of the Nineteenth U.S.C.T. in January 1864. He ended the war as a brigadier general, joined the Regular Army in 1866, and retired in 1891.

Thomas, Lorenzo (1804-1875), gained extensive experience in administration before and during the Mexican War. Early in the Civil War he became adjutant general of the army. Thomas played a major role in the organization of volunteers, especially the black regiments.

Thomas, William Widgery (1803-1884), referred to by Cyrus as Major Thomas, was a prominent businessman and politician in Portland, Maine. Louis C. Hatch, ed., *Maine: A History* (New York: American Historical Society, 1919), 4:49-50.

Tracy, Albert (1818-1893), was a Mexican War veteran and adjutant general of Maine from 1852 to 1855. He reenlisted as a captain in 1855 and joined Frémont's staff as an additional aide-de-camp with the rank of colonel in 1862. In 1863 and 1864, Tracy fought as a major in the Fifteenth U.S. Infantry. Brevetted lieutenant colonel in March 1865, he was retired for disability later that year. Francis F. Wayland, ed., "Frémont's Pursuit of Jackson in the Shenandoah Valley: The Journal of Colonel Albert Tracy, March-July 1862," *Virginia Magazine of History and Biography*, 70 (April 1962): 165-67.

Ullmann, Daniel (1810-1892), a New York City lawyer and politician, saw considerable action early in the war as colonel of the Seventy-eighth New York Volunteers. He fell ill and was taken prisoner at the Battle of Cedar Mountain. After being paroled, he urged Lincoln to emancipate the slaves and arm them as soldiers. Ullmann was commissioned brigadier general in January 1863, with orders to recruit a black brigade in Louisiana. After the fall of Port Hudson, he commanded that post and then the one at Morganza. In March 1865, he was brevetted major general and mustered out of service.

Van Nostrum. Possibly Abraham H. VanNostrand of the Fourth Wisconsin Volunteers. VanNostrand enlisted as a surgeon in 1861 and resigned in 1864. In July 1863, his regiment was in Baton Rouge, where there was an army hospital. *CWD*.

Varney, George (1834-1911), enlisted in May 1861 as a major in the Second Maine Infantry. He was promoted to lieutenant colonel in 1861 and colonel in 1863 and was mustered out with his regiment in 1863. *BBGB; CWD*.

Washburn, Israel, Jr. (1813-1883), had a distinguished career in the Maine legislature and Congress before the Civil War. He was the Republican governor of Maine in 1861 and 1862.

Wells, James M. (1808-1899), was born to a Louisiana planter family but educated largely in the North. An opponent of secession, he became lieutenant governor in Union-controlled Louisiana in 1864 and moved up to governor with Michael Hahn's election to the U.S. Senate. Wells shifted to the right for political reasons after Lincoln's assassination, but the intransigence of returning Confederate soldiers pushed him back to the radical Unionists. However, General Sheridan removed him from office in 1867 for not cooperating with the military authorities. Wells remained politically active until about 1880.

Wells, William R., as Acting Volunteer Lieutenant, commanded the USS *General Price*, which was stationed below Donaldsonville in 1864. U.S. Naval War Records Office, *Official Records of the Union and Confederate Navies in the War of the Rebellion*, ser. 1, vol. 26 (Washington, D.C.: GPO, 1914), 319, 554, 730.

Wentworth, Mark F. (1820-1897), a physician, was the captain of a militia company that occupied Fort McClary near Kittery, Maine, from April 30 to July 9, 1861. He enlisted as a lieutenant colonel in the Twenty-seventh Maine Infantry in 1862, was promoted to colonel, and later served as colonel of the Thirty-second Maine Infantry. *BBGB; CWD; OR*, ser. 3, vol. 1, pp. 663-64.

Wheeler, William H. (1817-1871), with John H. Lynde, published the *Bangor Daily Whig and Courier* with John H. Lynde. Joseph Griffin, ed., *History of the Press of Maine* (Brunswick, Me.: Press of J. Griffin, 1872), 133; *Zion's Herald*, April 2, 1874, p. 112.

Whittlesey, Elisha (1783-1863), served in Congress from 1823 to 1838 and subsequently in the U.S. Treasury. From 1849 to 1857 and again from 1861 to 1863, he was First Comptroller of the Treasury.

Wilson, Henry (1812-1875) was a Republican U.S. senator from Massachusetts from 1855 until 1873 and vice president of the United States from 1873 until 1875.

Wing, Horace M. (1838-1879), of the Eightieth U.S.C.T. was a second lieutenant and aide-de-camp on Cyrus's staff at Port Hudson. He was promoted to first lieutenant in August 1865. *CWD; OR*, ser. 1, vol. 48, pt. 1, p. 920; *OAR*, 257.

Wingate, John, was an ardent Republican from Bangor. The 1860 census lists a John J. Wingate as a 42-year-old blacksmith in Bangor, and there was a carriage-maker named John Wingate in Bangor in the 1850s. *L&T*, 2:350; William Farrand Prosser, *A History of the Puget Sound Country* (New York: Lewis Pub. Co., 1903), 2:545.

Wool, John E. (1784-1869), major general, commanded the Department of Virginia, the Middle Military Department, and the Department of the East before being retired on August 1, 1863.

Wright, George W. (1816-1885) was a merchant and banker in San Francisco and friend and business associate of Frémont. He and Frémont both belonged to California's first congressional delegation in 1850-1851. During the Civil War, Wright "was in and out of Washington lobbying on behalf of various persons and interests." Mary Lee Spence, "George W. Wright: Politician, Lobbyist, Entrepreneur," *Pacific Historical Review* 58 (August 1989): 345-59.

Yates, Richard (1815-1873), was the governor of Illinois during the Civil War and a Republican U.S. senator from 1865 to 1871.

Zulavsky, Ladislas L., was a Hungarian officer, nephew of the famous Hungarian patriot Kossuth, and one of four brothers in the Union army. Lieutenant colonel of the Fifth Regiment of the Ullmann Brigade, he later became colonel of the Eighty-seventh U.S.C.T. and commanded a black brigade in West Florida. Edmund Vasvary, *Lincoln's Hungarian Heroes: The Participation of Hungarians in the Civil War, 1861-1865* (Washington, D.C.: Hungarian Reformed Federation of America, 1939), 89; "UB", 296.

NOTES

1. I. S. Bangs, "The Ullman [*sic*] Brigade," in *War Papers Read Before the Commandery of the State of Maine, Military Order of the Loyal Legion of the United States*, 2 (Portland, Maine: Lefavor-Tower, 1902), 293.

2. *OR*, ser. 1, vol. 15, pp. 716-17.

3. *OR*, ser. 3, vol. 5, p. 120.

4. *OR*, ser. 1, vol. 26, pt. 1, p. 539.

5. *OR*, ser. 3, vol. 3, pp. 215-16.

6. *OR*, ser. 3, vol. 4, pp. 214-15. In the Department of the Gulf, twenty-two regiments of infantry, one each of engineers and cavalry, and one regiment and two battalions of heavy artillery had their designations changed from Corps d'Afrique to U.S.C.T. as of April 4, 1864.

Bibliographical Note

Like most men who die at twenty-eight, Cyrus Hamlin is too obscure a figure to have attracted the attention of historians and biographers. The entries in biographical encyclopedias are very brief and inaccurate. See *Appleton's Cyclopaedia of American Biography*, 3 (New York: D. Appleton, 1888), 366; *National Cyclopaedia of American Biography*, 5 (New York: James T. White, 1907), 422. Ezra Warner's *Generals in Blue* provides a more complete and more accurate summary of Cyrus's military service, but it still says very little about the man. A volume on Maine genealogy refers to Cyrus's "bravery at Cross Keyes" and states that he "helped to reconstruct the government of the state of Louisiana," leaving an impression of military prowess and political influence that is hardly justified by the record. George Thomas Little, ed., *Genealogical and Family History of the State of Maine* (New York: Lewis Historical Pub. Co., 1909), 1:9.

Aside from a few sentences in biographies of Hannibal Hamlin, nothing has been published on Cyrus's early life. However, these biographies provide some idea of the atmosphere in which Cyrus grew up. See Charles Eugene Hamlin, *The Life and Times of Hannibal Hamlin*, 2 vols. (1899; repr., Port Washington, N.Y.: Kennikat Press, 1971); H. Draper Hunt, *Hannibal Hamlin of Maine: Lincoln's First Vice President* (Syracuse: Syracuse University Press, 1969); and Mark Scroggins, *Hannibal: The Life of Abraham Lincoln's First Vice President* (Lanham, Md.: University Press of America, 1994). *History of Penobscot County, Maine* (Cleveland: Williams, Chase, 1882) offers information on Cyrus's hometown of Hampden, Maine. For insight into Cyrus's education, see Harriet Webster Marr, *The Old New England Academies Founded Before 1826* (New York: Comet Press, 1959). The Hamlin Family Papers include letters written by the teenaged Cyrus.

From the enormous literature on the Civil War and its aftermath, it is possible to select a few of the books and articles that are particularly relevant to Cyrus Hamlin's experiences. For thorough and vivid accounts of Stonewall Jackson's campaign in the Shenandoah Valley, during which Cyrus served on General Frémont's staff, see James I. Robertson, Jr., *Stonewall Jackson: The Man, the Soldier, the Legend* (New York: Macmillan Publishing USA, 1997), 323-457; Robert G. Tanner, *Stonewall in the Valley: Thomas J. "Stonewall" Jackson's Shenandoah Valley Campaign, Spring 1862*, rev. ed. (Mechanicsburg, Pa: Stackpole, 2002); and Peter Cozzens, *Shenandoah 1862: Stonewall Jackson's Valley Campaign* (Chapel Hill: University of North Carolina Press, 2008). For the perspective of Frémont and his staff, see Frémont's report of December 30, 1865, in *OR*, ser. 1, vol. 12, pt. 1, pp. 3-26; Francis F. Wayland, ed., "Frémont's Pursuit of Jackson in the Shenandoah Valley: The Journal of Colonel Albert Tracy, March-July 1862," *Virginia Magazine of History and Biography*, 70 (April and July 1962), 165-93, 332-54; and Allan Nevins, *Frémont: Pathmarker of the West*, (1955; repr., New York: Frederick Ungar, 1961), 2:550-63. Cozzens also presents a fairly sympathetic portrayal of Frémont.

Much has been written on the black military experience in the Civil War, but very little on the Ullmann Brigade, no doubt because it was slow to organize and saw no significant action. The first history of black soldiers in the Civil War by an African American, William Wells Brown, *The Negro in the American Rebellion: His Heroism and His Fidelity* (Boston: Lee & Shepard, 1867), does not mention Ullmann at all. In the 1880s, black historians George Washington Williams and Joseph T. Wilson, both Civil War veterans, published histories of the African American troops that contained only fleeting references to Ullmann and his regiments. See George W. Williams, *A History of the Negro Troops in the War of the Rebellion, 1861-1865* (New York: Harper & Bros., 1888) and Joseph T. Wilson, *The Black Phalanx: A History of the Negro Soldiers of the United States in the Wars of 1775-1812, 1861-'65* (Hartford: American Publishing Co., 1890). The standard introduction to the subject of black Union soldiers, first published in 1956, remains Dudley Taylor Cornish, *The Sable Arm: Black Troops in the Union Army, 1861-1865* (1956; repr., Lawrence: University Press of Kansas, 1987). Cornish pays a bit more attention to the Ullmann Brigade than do Williams, Wilson, and more recent books, such as John David Smith, ed., *Black Soldiers in Blue: African American Troops in the Civil War Era* (Chapel Hill: University of North Carolina Press, 2002) and Ira Berlin, ed., *Freedom: A Documentary History of Emancipation, 1861-1867*, ser. 2, *The Black Military Experience* (Cambridge, U.K.: Cambridge University Press, 1982). First-hand accounts of the Ullmann Brigade are Daniel Ullmann, *Address by Daniel Ullmann, L. L. D., before the Soldier's and Sailor's Union of the State of New York, on the Organization of Colored Troops and the Regeneration of the South* (Washington, D.C.: Great Republic, 1868) and I. S. Bangs, "The Ullman [*sic*] Brigade," in *War Papers Read*

Before the Commandery of the State of Maine, Military Order of the Loyal Legion of the United States, 2 (Portland, Me.: Lefavor-Tower, 1902): 289-310. Only about a third of Ullmann's address is devoted to his brigade, and even that is very general. Bangs provides more detail. See also David M. Gold, "Frustrated Glory: John Francis Appleton and Black Soldiers in the Civil War," *Maine Historical Society Quarterly*, 31 (Summer 1991): 174-204.

Modern studies of the relationship between white officers and the black soldiers they led include Joseph T. Glatthaar, *Forged in Battle: The Civil War Alliance of Black Soldiers and White Officers* (New York: Free Press, 1990) and Howard C. Westwood, *Black Troops, White Commanders, and Freedmen During the Civil War* (Carbondale: Southern Illinois University Press, 1992). For a comparison of the attitudes of three well-known commanders of black regiments toward their troops, see Keith Wilson, "In the Shadow of John Brown: The Military Service of Colonels Thomas Higginson, James Montgomery, and Robert Shaw in the Department of the South," in *Black Soldiers in Blue: African American Troops in the Civil War Era*, ed. John David Smith (Chapel Hill: University of North Carolina Press, 2002), 306-335.

Ted Tunnell, *Crucible of Reconstruction: War, Radicalism and Race in Louisiana, 1862-1877* (Baton Rouge: Louisiana State University Press, 1984) and Joe Gray Taylor, *Louisiana Reconstructed, 1863-1877* (Baton Rouge: Louisiana State University Press, 1974) cover Louisiana politics during Cyrus Hamlin's three years in New Orleans. James G. Hollandsworth, Jr., *An Absolute Massacre: The New Orleans Race Riot of July 30, 1866* (Baton Rouge: Louisiana State University Press, 2001) focuses more narrowly on the situation from 1864 to 1866, culminating in the New Orleans riot. James K. Hogue, *Uncivil War: Five New Orleans Street Battles and the Rise and Fall of Radical Reconstruction* (Baton Rouge: Louisiana State University Press, 2006), puts the 1866 riot in the context of both Louisiana politics and the series of violent outbreaks that occurred in New Orleans between 1866 and 1877.

On the epidemic that ended Cyrus Hamlin's life, see Jo Ann Carrigan, *The Saffron Scourge: A History of Yellow Fever in Louisiana, 1796-1905* (Lafayette, La.: Center for Louisiana Studies, University of Southwestern Louisiana, 1994), 97-101.

www.ingramcontent.com/pod-product-compliance
Lightning Source LLC
Chambersburg PA
CBHW070452090426
42735CB00012B/2518